AI Project Playbook From Concept to Deployment

Ikwe Gideon

Published by Ikwe Gideon, 2024.

AI PROJECT PLAYBOOK FROM CONCEPT TO DEPLOYMENT

First edition. December 8, 2024.

Written by Ikwe Gideon.

Table of Contents

Introduction

"Artificial Intelligence is the new electricity." – Andrew Ng

In today's fast-evolving world, Artificial Intelligence (AI) is driving unparalleled transformation. Across industries, AI is solving complex challenges, uncovering new opportunities, and reshaping the way organizations operate. Yet, while its potential is enormous, the path from concept to deployment is filled with intricate challenges. Successful AI projects demand careful planning, technical expertise, and seamless integration with strategic business goals.

This book, **AI Project Playbook: From Concept to Deployment**, is your ultimate guide for navigating the journey of AI project implementation. Whether you're a business leader, project manager, data scientist, or engineer, this playbook offers practical tools, actionable strategies, and real-world examples to help you execute AI projects with confidence and precision.

Why This Book?

Despite AI's transformative promise, many projects fall short of expectations due to common pitfalls—unclear objectives, unrealistic timelines, poor data strategies, and insufficient governance. This book directly addresses these challenges, providing a structured, end-to-end approach to managing AI projects. Grounded in industry best practices and real-world applications, it ensures you have the roadmap to turn AI concepts into scalable, impactful solutions.

What You Will Learn

Inside this playbook, you'll gain insights and expertise on:

1. **Inception and Planning:** Define business problems clearly, set realistic goals, and secure stakeholder alignment for AI success.
2. **Data Strategy and Preparation:** Develop high-quality data pipelines, implement governance frameworks, and optimize data for

model performance.

3. **Model Development and Deployment:** Choose the right algorithms, rigorously validate models, and deploy them efficiently at scale.
4. **Monitoring and Maintenance:** Build frameworks to detect model drift, maintain reliability, and ensure long-term performance.
5. **Governance and Compliance:** Navigate ethical considerations, regulatory compliance, and proactive risk management.
6. **Specialized Use Cases:** Explore advanced AI applications such as predictive analytics, fraud detection, and clinical decision support.

Who Is This Book For?

Whether you're new to AI projects or scaling existing solutions, this playbook is tailored for:

- **Business Leaders** looking to harness AI for strategic innovation and ROI.
- **Data Scientists and Engineers** seeking detailed workflows for enterprise-level AI projects.
- **Project Managers** managing multidisciplinary teams through complex AI lifecycles.
- **Technical Teams** focused on building scalable, secure, and compliant AI systems.

No matter your role, this book equips you with the insights to overcome challenges and achieve impactful results.

How This Book Is Structured

The book is organized to guide you seamlessly through the AI lifecycle, covering:

- **Conceptual Foundations:** Understanding the principles behind each phase.
- **Practical Frameworks:** Actionable templates, checklists, and

workflows.

- **Real-World Case Studies:** Examples from diverse industries illustrating best practices.
- **Hands-On Exercises:** Practical steps to immediately apply your knowledge.

Each chapter builds on the last, starting with foundational planning and advancing through data strategy, model development, deployment, and beyond. Together, they provide an actionable roadmap for successful AI implementation.

The Future of AI Implementation

As AI continues to evolve, its impact on industries and society will depend on thoughtful design, ethical practices, and effective execution. This playbook not only addresses the technical and operational aspects of AI but also emphasizes governance, compliance, and sustainability.

Embark on this journey to master AI project implementation. Whether you're building your first AI solution or scaling advanced applications, this book is your trusted companion for delivering value-driven, scalable, and ethical AI solutions.

Welcome to the **AI Project Playbook: From Concept to Deployment**—your roadmap to AI success begins here.

Chapter 1: Project Inception and Planning

"Plans are worthless, but planning is everything." – Dwight D. Eisenhower

The journey of implementing an artificial intelligence solution begins long before the first line of code is written. Success in AI projects hinges on thorough planning, clear problem definition, and strategic stakeholder alignment. This chapter will guide you through the critical initial phases that set the foundation for your AI project's success.

1.1 Problem Definition

Understanding the Business Need

The most successful AI projects begin with a clear understanding of the business problem they aim to solve. AI should not be implemented for its own sake; the technology must address a specific, valuable need.

Example Scenario:

A retail company approaches your team wanting to "implement AI." This vague request needs to be refined into a specific problem statement, such as:

"Predict inventory requirements for each store location to reduce stockouts by 30% while minimizing excess inventory costs."

Key Questions to Ask:

- What specific business problem are we trying to solve?
- Why is this problem important to the organization?
- What are the current solutions or workarounds?
- How will we measure success?
- What is the estimated business value of solving this problem?

Defining Project Scope

Scope creep is one of the primary reasons AI projects fail. Clear boundaries must be established early to ensure project success.

Example Scope Definition Template:

Project Goal: [Clear, measurable objective]

In Scope:

- [Specific feature/functionality 1]
- [Specific feature/functionality 2]

Out of Scope:

- [Excluded feature/functionality 1]
- [Excluded feature/functionality 2]

Dependencies:

- [Required resource/system 1]
- [Required resource/system 2]

Setting Success Criteria

Success criteria should be SMART (Specific, Measurable, Achievable, Relevant, Time-bound).

Example Success Criteria for Retail Inventory Project:

Primary Metrics:

1. Reduce stockouts by 30% within six months of deployment
2. Decrease excess inventory costs by 20%
3. Achieve 85% prediction accuracy for weekly inventory needs

Secondary Metrics:

1. System response time under 500ms for predictions
2. 99.9% system uptime
3. User adoption rate of 90% among store managers

Feasibility Assessment

Before proceeding, assess the project's feasibility across multiple dimensions:

1. Technical Feasibility

- Do we have access to the required data?
- Is the quality and quantity of data sufficient?
- Do we have the necessary technical expertise?
- Are our infrastructure and tools adequate?

2. Business Feasibility

- Does the expected ROI justify the investment?
- Do we have stakeholder buy-in?
- Are there regulatory or compliance concerns?
- Do we have access to necessary resources?

3. Operational Feasibility

- Can the solution be integrated into existing workflows?
- Do we have the operational capacity to maintain the solution?
- Is the timeline realistic?
- Are there change management considerations?

Resource Estimation

1. Human Resources:

- Data Scientists: [Number needed and duration]
- ML Engineers: [Number needed and duration]
- DevOps Engineers: [Number needed and duration]
- Project Manager: [Allocation percentage]
- Domain Experts: [Availability requirements]

2. Technical Resources:

- Computing Infrastructure
- Storage Requirements
- Development Tools

- Testing Environment
- Production Environment

3. Data Resources:

- Data Collection Costs
- Data Labeling Resources
- Data Storage
- Data Processing Capacity

4. Timeline Estimation:

Phase	Duration
Problem Definition	2–3 weeks
Data Collection & Preparation	4–6 weeks
Model Development	8–12 weeks
Testing & Validation	4–6 weeks
Deployment & Integration	4–6 weeks

Common Pitfalls to Avoid

1. **Unclear Problem Definition**
   - **Impact:** Scope creep, misaligned expectations
   - **Solution:** Invest time in detailed problem definition and documentation
2. **Insufficient Data Assessment**
   - **Impact:** Model performance issues, project delays
   - **Solution:** Conduct thorough data availability and quality assessments early
3. **Unrealistic Expectations**
   - **Impact:** Stakeholder disappointment, project failure
   - **Solution:** Set clear, achievable goals based on available resources
4. **Inadequate Resource Planning**
   - **Impact:** Project delays, budget overruns

- **Solution:** Conduct detailed resource planning with contingency

Practical Exercise

Create a comprehensive project charter for an AI initiative, including:

1. Problem statement
2. Scope definition
3. Success criteria
4. Resource requirements
5. Initial timeline
6. Risk assessment

1.2 Stakeholder Management

Identifying Key Stakeholders

Successful AI projects require support and alignment from multiple stakeholders across the organization.

Stakeholder Matrix

Influence Level	High Interest	Low Interest
High Power	Manage Closely	Keep Satisfied
Low Power	Keep Informed	Monitor

Common Stakeholders Include:

1. **Executive Sponsors**
   - C-level executives, department heads, budget controllers
2. **Technical Teams**
   - Data scientists, ML engineers, DevOps teams, IT infrastructure teams
3. **Business Users**
   - End users, department managers, operations teams
4. **Support Functions**
   - Legal/compliance, security teams, HR, training teams

Communication Planning

Communication Framework:

Stakeholder Group	Communication Method	Frequency	Key Information
Executive Sponsors	Executive Summary	Bi-weekly	Project status, KPIs, risks
Technical Teams	Detailed Reports	Weekly	Technical progress, challenges
Business Users	Updates & Training	Monthly	Features, benefits, training
Support Functions	Compliance Reports	As needed	Security, legal requirements

1.3 Project Planning

Timeline Development

Phase 1: Project Setup (Weeks 1–3)

- **Week 1:** Stakeholder interviews, problem definition refinement, initial team assembly
- **Week 2:** Data assessment, infrastructure planning, initial project charter
- **Week 3:** Stakeholder sign-off, resource allocation, project kickoff

Phase 2: Data Preparation (Weeks 4–9)

- **Weeks 4–5:** Data collection, quality assessment, initial cleaning scripts
- **Weeks 6–7:** Feature engineering, data pipeline development, quality validation
- **Weeks 8–9:** Data documentation, pipeline testing, initial baseline metrics

Resource Allocation

Core Team:

- Project Manager (100%)
- Lead Data Scientist (100%)
- ML Engineers (2 x 100%)
- DevOps Engineer (50%)
- Domain Expert (25%)

Support Team:

- Business Analyst (50%)
- QA Engineer (50%)
- UI/UX Designer (25%)

Risk Management

Risk Assessment Matrix:

Risk Category	Probability	Impact	Mitigation Strategy
Data Quality	High	High	Early validation, cleanup procedures
Technical Complexity	Medium	High	POC phase, expert consultation
Resource Availability	Medium	Medium	Cross-training, backup resources
Stakeholder Alignment	Low	High	Regular communication, clear documentation

Chapter Summary

The success of an AI project heavily depends on:

1. Identifying and categorizing stakeholders early
2. Developing clear communication strategies
3. Creating detailed project timelines
4. Allocating resources appropriately
5. Implementing robust governance structures
6. Planning for risk management

7. Establishing quality control measures

Chapter 2: Data Strategy and Collection

In the world of real-world AI projects, data collection is rarely a blank slate. Most organizations already possess a wealth of existing data sources, systems, and processes, often spread across departments or embedded in legacy infrastructure. This chapter delves into the foundational principles of data strategy and practical approaches to data collection in enterprise settings. By the end of this chapter, you'll have a clearer understanding of how to navigate, optimize, and leverage enterprise data landscapes for AI success.

2.1 Understanding Your Data Landscape

Enterprise Data Sources

Organizations rely on a variety of data systems, each serving different operational and strategic needs. Here are the most common categories:

1. Internal Systems

- **Customer Relationship Management (CRM):**
  These platforms track customer interactions, sales pipelines, and account management, providing valuable insights for AI models. Examples include:
  - **Salesforce:** Industry leader in CRM with robust customization.
  - **Microsoft Dynamics:** Integrated with other Microsoft tools for seamless workflows.
  - **HubSpot:** Widely used for inbound marketing and sales management.
- **Enterprise Resource Planning (ERP):**
  ERP systems are the backbone of enterprise operations, managing everything from finance to supply chains. Examples:
  - **SAP:** Known for comprehensive enterprise management solutions.
  - **Oracle:** Powerful ERP with analytics capabilities.
  - **Microsoft Dynamics 365:** Flexible and cloud-friendly ERP software.
- **Human Resources Information Systems (HRIS):**
  These platforms streamline HR processes and provide workforce data

critical for AI in HR applications:
  - **Workday:** A leader in HRIS with predictive analytics features.
  - **ADP:** Well-suited for payroll and compliance needs.
  - **BambooHR:** Focused on small to mid-sized businesses.

2. Digital Platforms

- **Website Analytics:**
  These tools provide insights into web traffic and user behavior, vital for customer-centric AI models:
  - **Google Analytics:** Industry-standard for tracking website performance.
  - **Adobe Analytics:** Advanced segmentation and reporting capabilities.
  - **Mixpanel:** Focuses on user behavior analytics.
- **Marketing Platforms:**
  Collecting and analyzing marketing data helps fine-tune campaigns and personalize customer experiences:
  - **Mailchimp:** Popular for email marketing automation.
  - **HubSpot:** An all-in-one platform for marketing and sales.
  - **Marketo:** Tailored for large-scale marketing automation.
- **Social Media Management:**
  Social platforms offer a treasure trove of customer sentiment and engagement data:
  - **Sprinklr:** Comprehensive platform for social listening and management.
  - **Hootsuite:** Easy-to-use scheduling and analytics tools.
  - **Buffer:** Focused on streamlined post scheduling.

3. Operational Systems

- **Point of Sale (POS):** Tracks sales transactions, essential for retail analytics.
- **Inventory Management:** Optimizes stock levels and supply chain efficiency.
- **Customer Service Platforms:** Monitors support tickets and resolutions.

- **IoT Devices and Sensors:** Provides real-time operational data from connected devices.

Data Access Methods

Once data sources are identified, determining how to access this data efficiently is crucial. Here are the most common methods:

1. Direct Database Access

- SQL databases for structured queries.
- NoSQL databases for flexible, unstructured data.
- Data warehouses such as Snowflake, Redshift, and BigQuery for analytics.

2. API Integration

- **REST APIs:** Lightweight and widely used.
- **GraphQL:** Query-specific data fetching.
- **SOAP Services:** Enterprise-grade, secure integrations.

3. File Exports

- CSV dumps for straightforward data sharing.
- Excel reports for tabular formats.
- JSON exports for web-friendly data.

4. ETL Tools

- **Informatica:** Scalable enterprise-grade ETL.
- **Talend:** Open-source and flexible.
- **Apache NiFi:** Real-time data flow automation.

2.2 Data Collection Strategy

Assessment Phase

Before collecting data, organizations should evaluate their existing systems. This phase involves:

1. Data Inventory

A thorough inventory provides a comprehensive view of available data. Key actions include:

- Listing all potential data sources.
- Documenting data owners for accountability.
- Identifying data formats for compatibility.
- Mapping data refresh frequencies for planning updates.

Example Data Inventory Table:

Source System	Data Owner	Format	Refresh Rate	Access Method
Salesforce	Sales Ops	API	Real-time	API Token
SAP ERP	IT	Database	Daily	Direct SQL
GA4	Marketing	API	Hourly	OAuth 2.0

2. Data Quality Assessment

Assess the usability of your data by evaluating:

- Completeness of records.
- Accuracy of values.
- Consistency across systems.
- Historical availability for trend analysis.

3. Access Requirements

Identify and document:

- Security clearances.
- API credentials and configurations.
- Database permissions.
- Data sharing agreements for compliance.

Common Challenges and Solutions

1. **Data Silos**
    - **Challenge:** Disjointed data across departments.
    - **Solution:** Create a centralized data catalog and facilitate access through governance frameworks.
2. **Inconsistent Formats**
    - **Challenge:** Varying data formats hinder integration.
    - **Solution:** Implement data standardization within the data warehouse.
3. **Access Restrictions**
    - **Challenge:** Compliance and security constraints limit data sharing.
    - **Solution:** Establish robust data governance policies to ensure secure, compliant access.

2.3 Practical Implementation

Case Study: Customer Churn Prediction

Step 1: Data Requirements

Business Question: "Which customers are likely to churn in the next three months?"

Required Data Points:

- **Customer Information:** Demographics, contract details, billing history.
- **Product Usage:** Login frequency, feature adoption, support tickets.
- **Communication History:** Email engagement, support interactions, survey responses.

Step 2: Source System Mapping

Data Point	Source System	Access Method	Update Frequency
Demographics	Salesforce	API	Daily
Billing	SAP	Database	Daily
Usage	Product Analytics	API	Hourly
Support	Zendesk	API	Real-time
Email	Mailchimp	API	Daily

Step 3: Implementation Plan

Data Collection Process:

- **Morning ETL Jobs:**
  - 2:00 AM: SAP billing data export.
  - 3:00 AM: Salesforce daily sync.
  - 4:00 AM: Email engagement update.
  - 5:00 AM: Data warehouse refresh.
- **Real-Time Streams:**
  - Product usage events.
  - Support ticket creation.
  - Customer interactions.

System Integration:

- **Data Warehouse:** Snowflake.
- **ETL Tool:** Informatica.
- **Stream Processing:** Kafka.

Step 4: Data Quality Monitoring

- **Daily Checks:** Record counts, missing values, value ranges, update timestamps.
- **Weekly Reviews:** Trends, system performance, error patterns.

Best Practices

1. **Documentation**
    - Maintain a data dictionary and source system details.
    - Document access procedures and update schedules.
2. **Governance**
    - Assign data ownership.
    - Define access controls and compliance policies.
3. **Monitoring**
    - Track system health and data quality.
    - Monitor usage patterns and associated costs.

2.4 Real-World Considerations

Cost Management

1. **Storage Costs:** Optimize data warehouse usage and backup solutions.
2. **Processing Costs:** Streamline ETL and real-time processes.
3. **Access Costs:** Manage API call charges and licensing fees.

Compliance Requirements

1. **Data Privacy:** Ensure adherence to GDPR, CCPA, and industry regulations.
2. **Security:** Enforce encryption, access control, and audit logging.
3. **Retention:** Define archival and deletion policies aligned with organizational needs.

Practical Exercises

1. **Data Inventory Exercise:** Create a data inventory, identify gaps, and document access methods.
2. **Integration Planning:** Map data flows, define transformation rules, and plan refresh schedules.
3. **Quality Framework:** Define metrics, create monitoring dashboards, and establish alert thresholds.

Chapter Summary

- Start with existing data sources and assess their utility.
- Map data requirements to the most relevant systems.
- Develop integration strategies to ensure seamless data flows.
- Establish robust quality monitoring practices.
- Manage costs and ensure compliance with regulations.
- Document every process for clarity and consistency.

By focusing on these core strategies, enterprises can build a solid foundation for data-driven AI initiatives.

Chapter 3: Data Preparation and Feature Engineering

Data preparation often accounts for 60-80% of the time spent on AI projects. It is the bedrock of successful AI systems, transforming raw data into a form that models can effectively use. Feature engineering further enhances the data by extracting valuable insights that drive predictive power. This chapter provides a comprehensive guide to practical approaches in data preparation and feature engineering, leveraging common enterprise tools and workflows.

3.1 Data Preparation Fundamentals

Understanding Your Data Warehouse

Modern enterprises typically rely on robust data warehouses to manage and process vast datasets. Common platforms include:

- **Snowflake**: Highly scalable and cloud-native.
- **Amazon Redshift**: Optimized for analytics on AWS.
- **Google BigQuery**: Known for its serverless architecture.
- **Azure Synapse**: Integrated with Microsoft's ecosystem.

Key Concepts

1. **Data Loading Zones**
    - **Raw/Bronze Layer:** Stores an unaltered copy of source data.
    - **Silver Layer:** Contains cleaned, standardized data.
    - **Gold Layer:** Business-ready data, enriched and transformed for specific use cases.
2. **Common Table Types**
    - **Staging Tables:** Temporary tables for processing.
    - **Dimension Tables:** Hold descriptive attributes (e.g., customers, products).
    - **Fact Tables:** Store measurable business events (e.g., sales

transactions).
    - **Aggregate Tables:** Summarize data for quick reporting.

Real-World Example: E-commerce Data Structure

For an e-commerce company, data might be structured as follows:

—Bronze layer: raw transaction data

TRANSACTIONS_RAW

—Silver layer: cleaned transaction data

TRANSACTIONS_CLEAN

—Gold layer: enriched with customer insights

TRANSACTIONS_ENRICHED

—Customer reference data

CUSTOMER_DIMENSION

—Product reference data

PRODUCT_DIMENSION

3.2 Data Cleaning

Common Data Quality Issues

1. **Missing Values**
    - **Example:** Missing customer age in CRM systems.
    - **Solution:** Estimate age using title (e.g., Mr., Ms., Dr.).
    - **Tool:** Use **Alteryx** for automated bulk updates.
2. **Inconsistent Formats**
    - **Example:** Phone numbers recorded in various formats.
    - **Solution:** Standardize formats to E.164.
    - **Tool:** Apply transformations in **dbt**.
3. **Duplicate Records**

- **Example:** Multiple records for the same customer across systems.
- **Solution:** Use survivorship rules to create a "golden record."
- **Tool:** Leverage **Informatica MDM** for deduplication.

Practical Cleaning Workflow

1. **Profile Data**
    - **Tool:** Informatica Data Quality.
    - **Tasks:** Analyze value distributions, patterns, and anomalies.
    - **Output:** Document issues in a data quality dashboard.
2. **Define Business Rules**

Rule	Description	Action
Valid Email	Must contain "@"	Flag invalid emails
Age Range	18-100 years	Cap outliers
Product Price	> $0	Remove invalid prices

1. **Implement Cleaning Logic**
    - Apply SQL transformations in the data warehouse.
    - Use ETL tools to enforce rules.
    - Document all changes for reproducibility.

3.3 Feature Engineering

Types of Features

1. **Temporal Features**
    - **Use Case:** Calculate customer lifetime value or purchase frequency.
    - **Example in Retail:**

SELECT

customer_id,

DATEDIFF(day, last_purchase_date, CURRENT_DATE) AS days_since_last_purchase,

COUNT(order_id)/DATEDIFF(day, first_purchase_date, CURRENT_DATE) AS purchase_frequency

FROM customer_transactions

1. **Categorical Features**
    - **Use Case:** Classify customers into segments or products into categories.
    - **Example in Banking:**

CASE

WHEN avg_balance > 100000 THEN 'Premium'

WHEN avg_balance > 50000 THEN 'Gold'

ELSE 'Standard'

END AS customer_segment

1. **Behavioral Features**
    - **Use Case:** Analyze customer habits such as browse-to-buy ratios or cart abandonment rates.

Feature Engineering Process

1. **Domain Expert Consultation**
    - Collaborate with business experts to understand key indicators.
    - **Example Workshop Questions:**
        - What traits define high-value customers?
        - What behaviors predict churn?
2. **Feature Creation**
    - **Common Tools:**

        - **dbt**: SQL transformations.
        - **Alteryx**: Visual workflows.
        - **Python**: Advanced calculations.
    - **Example Schema:**

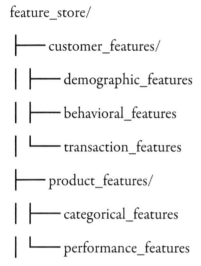

```
feature_store/
├── customer_features/
│   ├── demographic_features
│   ├── behavioral_features
│   └── transaction_features
├── product_features/
│   ├── categorical_features
│   └── performance_features
```

1. **Feature Validation**
    - Ensure logical correctness, data freshness, and completeness.
    - Validate distributions and monitor for anomalies.

3.4 Practical Implementation Guide

Case Study: Customer Churn Prevention

1. **Initial Data Assessment**
   Review and map key data sources:

Source	Table	Key Fields	Update Frequency
CRM	Customers	Demographics	Daily
Transactions	Orders	Purchase history	Real-time
Product	Usage	Activity logs	Hourly

1. **Data Preparation Steps**

- Load raw data into the bronze layer.
- Apply standardization and cleaning rules.
- Merge duplicate records and resolve missing values.
- Create business-ready gold layer views.

2. **Feature Engineering**
   Focus on:
   - **Customer Engagement:** Login frequency, feature usage, support ticket counts.
   - **Financial Indicators:** Revenue trends, payment patterns, contract values.
   - **Risk Indicators:** Service disruptions, complaints, competitor interactions.
3. **Implementation Schedule**

Day	Task
Monday	Data refresh and cleaning
Tuesday	Feature calculation
Wednesday	Quality checks
Thursday	Business review
Friday	Updates and fixes

3.5 Best Practices

Documentation

1. Maintain a comprehensive data dictionary.
2. Record all transformation rules, including versions and rationale.
3. Track quality metrics like completeness, accuracy, and timeliness.

Governance

1. Implement strict access controls and audit logging.
2. Use version control for features and transformation logic.
3. Monitor data health with quality dashboards and alerts.

Monitoring

1. Establish daily and weekly checks for quality and system performance.
2. Track feature usage to assess relevance and impact.

Practical Exercises

1. **Data Profiling Exercise:** Analyze source tables, identify issues, and document findings.
2. **Feature Creation Exercise:** Select a business problem, design features, and implement them.
3. **Quality Monitoring Exercise:** Create dashboards, set alerts, and track metrics.

Chapter Summary

- Thoroughly understand the data warehouse and its zones.
- Identify and resolve data quality issues systematically.
- Focus on features that align with business goals.
- Leverage tools for robust transformations and validations.
- Continuously document and monitor processes for long-term success.

This structured approach ensures a strong foundation for building reliable and impactful AI systems.

Chapter 4: Model Development and Deployment

In enterprise environments, model development is about more than just selecting the right algorithms—it's about building sustainable, production-ready solutions that integrate seamlessly with existing systems. This chapter explores the practical approaches to developing and deploying machine learning models in corporate settings, focusing on infrastructure, workflows, validation, deployment, and operational excellence.

4.1 Setting Up the Development Environment

Enterprise ML Infrastructure

1. Common Development Platforms

- **Azure Machine Learning**
- **AWS SageMaker**
- **Google Vertex AI**
- **Databricks**

2. Development Environment Components

Component	Common Tools	Purpose
Notebooks	Jupyter Enterprise Gateway	Experimentation
Version Control	GitLab/GitHub Enterprise	Code management
Package Management	Artifactory	Library control
Compute Resources	Kubernetes clusters	Training/inference

3. Access and Security

- **SSO Integration:** Simplifies login and enhances security.
- **Role-Based Access Control:** Ensures appropriate access for users.
- **Audit Logging:** Tracks user actions for compliance.
- **Secret Management:** Protects sensitive credentials.

4.2 Model Development Process

Phase 1: Baseline Model Development

1. **Project Setup**

Organize your project for clarity and scalability:

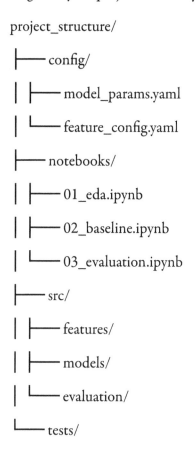

```
project_structure/
├── config/
│   ├── model_params.yaml
│   └── feature_config.yaml
├── notebooks/
│   ├── 01_eda.ipynb
│   ├── 02_baseline.ipynb
│   └── 03_evaluation.ipynb
├── src/
│   ├── features/
│   ├── models/
│   └── evaluation/
└── tests/
```

1. **Model Selection Strategy**

Model Type	Use Case	Pros	Cons
Random Forest	Customer Segmentation	Interpretable, robust	Resource heavy
XGBoost	Churn Prediction	High performance	Complex tuning
Linear Models	Risk Scoring	Simple, fast	Limited complexity

1. **Development Workflow**

- Pull the latest data from the feature store.
- Train a baseline model.
- Log metrics to a tracking system (e.g., MLflow).
- Review results with business stakeholders.
- Iterate based on feedback.

Phase 2: Model Refinement

1. **Experimentation Management**

Experiment	Features	Parameters	Metrics
exp_001	base_features	default_params	auc=0.82
exp_002	+derived_features	tuned_params	auc=0.85
exp_003	+external_data	optimized_params	auc=0.87

1. **Hyperparameter Optimization**

- **Grid Search:** Ideal for simple models.
- **Bayesian Optimization:** Suited for complex models.
- **Cross-Validation Strategies:** Ensures robust evaluation.

1. **Business Metric Alignment**

Business Metric	Model Metric	Target
Customer Retention	AUC-ROC	> 0.85
Campaign Efficiency	Precision@K	> 0.70
Risk Reduction	False Positive Rate	< 0.10

4.3 Model Validation

Business Validation

1. **Stakeholder Review Process**

- Week 1: Technical validation.
- Week 2: Business review.
- Week 3: Compliance review.
- Week 4: Final approval.

1. **Performance Criteria**

Criteria	Threshold	Current	Status
Model Accuracy	85%	87%	Pass �
Inference Time	<100ms	80ms	Pass �
Bias Metrics	<0.05	0.03	Pass �

Technical Validation

1. **Testing Framework**

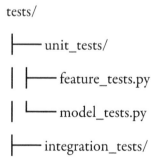

```
tests/
├── unit_tests/
│   ├── feature_tests.py
│   └── model_tests.py
├── integration_tests/
```

```
│ ├── pipeline_tests.py
│ └── api_tests.py
└── performance_tests/
├── load_tests.py
└── stress_tests.py
```

1. **Quality Gates**

- Code coverage > 80%.
- Performance benchmarks met.
- All tests passing.
- Documentation complete.

4.4 Model Deployment

Deployment Strategies

Pattern	Use Case	Pros	Cons
Shadow Mode	New Models	Safe validation	Resource intensive
A/B Testing	Incremental Updates	Measured impact	Complex setup
Canary	Critical Systems	Risk management	Slower rollout

Infrastructure Requirements

```
Production Environment/
├── Model Service (Kubernetes)
│ ├── Primary Pod
│ └── Backup Pod
├── Monitoring (Prometheus)
├── Logging (ELK Stack)
```

└── Load Balancer

Real-World Deployment Example

Case Study: Credit Risk Model Deployment

1. **Pre-Deployment Checklist**

- Model cards complete.
- API documentation ready.
- Performance benchmarks met.
- Compliance review passed.
- Rollback plan documented.

1. **Deployment Schedule**

- Week 1: Deploy to UAT.
- Week 2: Limited production release (5% traffic).
- Week 3: Gradual traffic increase.
- Week 4: Full production deployment.

1. **Monitoring Setup**

Dashboard Components:

- Model performance metrics.
- System health metrics.
- Business impact metrics.
- Alert thresholds.

4.5 Operational Excellence

Production Monitoring

Category	Metric	Threshold	Alert
Performance	Response Time	<100ms	>200ms
Quality	Prediction Drift	<5%	>10%
System	CPU Usage	<70%	>85%

Incident Response

Incident Severity Levels:

- **P0:** Model critical failure.
- **P1:** Performance degradation.
- **P2:** Minor issues.

Maintenance Procedures

1. **Regular Updates:**
    - Daily: Metric checks.
    - Weekly: Performance reviews.
    - Monthly: Model retraining.
    - Quarterly: Major version updates.
2. **Documentation Requirements:**
    - Model cards.
    - API specifications.
    - Runbooks.
    - Training manuals.

4.6 Compliance and Governance

Model Governance

Field	Description	Example
Model ID	Unique identifier	RISK_MODEL_001
Version	Current version	v2.1.0
Status	Deployment status	PROD
Owner	Responsible team	Risk Analytics

Audit Requirements

- Model validation reports.
- Performance history.
- Change logs.
- Access records.

Practical Exercises

1. **Development Exercise:**
    - Set up the development environment.
    - Train a baseline model.
    - Document the process.
2. **Deployment Exercise:**
    - Create a deployment plan.
    - Set up monitoring systems.
    - Implement rollback procedures.
3. **Operations Exercise:**
    - Monitor a production model.
    - Handle common issues.
    - Update documentation.

Chapter Summary

- Establish proper development infrastructure.
- Follow a structured model development process.
- Validate models through rigorous business and technical reviews.
- Deploy with careful planning and monitoring.
- Maintain operational excellence through regular updates and governance.
- Ensure compliance and transparency with robust documentation and auditability.

This chapter equips you with the tools and strategies to develop and deploy AI models effectively in enterprise settings.

Chapter 5: Model Monitoring and Maintenance

In production environments, the performance and value of machine learning models hinge on effective monitoring and maintenance. This chapter provides practical strategies for implementing robust monitoring systems, managing alerts, maintaining models, and optimizing costs in enterprise settings.

5.1 Setting Up Monitoring Infrastructure

Enterprise Monitoring Stack

1. Common Monitoring Platforms

Tool	Purpose	Common Use Cases
Prometheus	Metrics collection	System metrics
Grafana	Visualization	Real-time dashboards
ELK Stack	Log analysis	Error tracking
DataDog	Application monitoring	Performance monitoring
WhyLabs	ML monitoring	Data drift detection

2. Monitoring Architecture

```
Production Environment/
├── Model Service
│   ├── Application Metrics
│   ├── Business Metrics
│   └── ML Metrics
├── Monitoring Service
│   ├── Metric Collection
│   ├── Alert Management
```

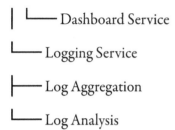

│ └── Dashboard Service

└── Logging Service

├── Log Aggregation

└── Log Analysis

5.2 Key Monitoring Areas

1. Data Quality Monitoring

Metric	Description	Threshold	Action
Missing Values	% of null values	>5%	Alert Data Team
Data Freshness	Time since last update	>24h	Check pipeline
Schema Changes	Column modifications	Any change	Review impact
Value Range	Outside expected bounds	>3σ	Investigate

Example Dashboard Layout

Data Quality Dashboard/

├── Data Completeness

│ ├── Missing Value Trends

│ └── Field Completion Rates

├── Data Freshness

│ ├── Last Update Times

│ └── Delay Tracking

└── Data Validation

├── Schema Compliance

└── Value Distribution

2. Model Performance Monitoring

Technical Metrics

Metric	Tool	Alert Threshold
Accuracy	MLflow	<85%
Latency	Prometheus	>100ms
Error Rate	DataDog	>1%
CPU Usage	Grafana	>80%

Business Metrics

Retail Example:

Metric	Description	Target	Current
Revenue Impact	Additional revenue	$100K/month	$95K
Customer Satisfaction	CSAT score	>4.5	4.3
Operation Efficiency	Time saved	20hrs/week	18hrs

3. Drift Monitoring

Types of Drift

1. **Data Drift**
   - Monitor: Feature distributions, input patterns, data quality metrics.
   - Tools: Evidently AI, WhyLabs, Amazon SageMaker Model Monitor.
2. **Concept Drift**
   - Monitor: Model performance metrics, business KPI correlation, prediction distributions.
   - Frequency:
     - Daily: Performance checks.
     - Weekly: Distribution analysis.
     - Monthly: Deep-dive reviews.

5.3 Alert Management

Alert Framework

1. Severity Levels

Level	Description	Response Time	Example
P0	Critical	15 minutes	Model down
P1	High	1 hour	Performance degradation
P2	Medium	4 hours	Minor drift
P3	Low	24 hours	Documentation update

2. Alert Routing

Alert Flow:

1. **Detection:** Monitoring system flags an issue.
2. **Classification:** Alert Manager categorizes severity.
3. **Notification:** Tools like PagerDuty or Slack notify stakeholders.
4. **Assignment:** Incident assigned via JIRA or ServiceNow.
5. **Resolution Tracking:** Progress monitored until resolved.

Example Alert Runbook

Scenario: Performance Degradation Alert

1. **Initial Assessment (15 mins):**
   - Check dashboard metrics.
   - Verify alert legitimacy.
   - Assess business impact.
2. **Investigation (1 hour):**
   - Review recent changes.
   - Check data quality.
   - Analyze error patterns.
3. **Resolution (2 hours):**
   - Implement fix.
   - Verify improvement.
   - Document incident.
4. **Follow-up (24 hours):**
   - Conduct root cause analysis.
   - Update monitoring protocols.

- Develop preventive measures.

5.4 Regular Maintenance

Maintenance Schedule

1. **Daily Tasks:**
   - Monitor key metrics.
   - Review alerts.
   - Check data pipeline health.
   - Verify prediction quality.
2. **Weekly Tasks:**
   - Analyze performance trends.
   - Report to stakeholders.
   - Optimize resources.
   - Review error patterns.
3. **Monthly Tasks:**
   - Conduct comprehensive model reviews.
   - Assess retraining needs.
   - Plan capacity upgrades.
   - Update documentation.
4. **Quarterly Tasks:**
   - Perform major version updates.
   - Review infrastructure.
   - Conduct compliance audits.
   - Optimize costs.

Model Retraining Strategy

Trigger	Threshold	Action
Performance Drop	>5%	Investigate
Data Drift	>10%	Retrain
Time-Based	Every 3 months	Review
Business Change	Any significant change	Assess

Retraining Process

1. **Data Preparation:**
   - Collect new data.
   - Validate data quality.
   - Update features.
2. **Model Update:**
   - Train a new version.
   - Validate performance.
   - Compare with current model.
3. **Deployment:**
   - Stage new model.
   - Conduct A/B testing.
   - Roll out gradually.

5.5 Documentation and Reporting

Required Documentation

1. **Model Cards**

Template:

- Model Overview
- Performance Metrics
- Training Data Details
- Limitations
- Maintenance Requirements

1. **Monitoring Documentation**
   - Metric definitions.
   - Alert thresholds.
   - Response procedures.
   - Contact information.
2. **Regular Reports**

Report	Frequency	Audience	Content
Health Check	Daily	Technical	Metrics
Performance	Weekly	Business	KPIs
Review	Monthly	Stakeholders	Summary
Audit	Quarterly	Compliance	Full Review

5.6 Cost Management

Monitoring Costs

Component	Cost Driver	Optimization
Storage	Log retention	Implement cleanup policy
Compute	Query frequency	Aggregate data
Tools	License fees	Review usage regularly

Cost Optimization Strategies

1. Right-size resources.
2. Optimize retention policies.
3. Review tool licenses and usage.
4. Automate cleanup processes.

Practical Exercises

1. **Monitoring Setup Exercise:**
    - Configure basic monitoring tools.
    - Set up alerts.
    - Design dashboards.
2. **Incident Response Exercise:**
    - Simulate a common issue.
    - Practice response workflows.
    - Document lessons learned.
3. **Maintenance Exercise:**
    - Create a maintenance schedule.
    - Implement regular checks.
    - Update procedures and documentation.

Chapter Summary

- Establish a comprehensive monitoring infrastructure.
- Monitor data quality, model performance, and drift continuously.
- Implement a robust alert management framework.
- Maintain regular schedules for checks, retraining, and updates.
- Document and report processes effectively.
- Manage costs through optimization strategies.

By focusing on these principles, organizations can ensure the reliability, performance, and business impact of their machine learning systems over time.

Chapter 6: Model Governance and Compliance

In enterprise environments, AI governance and compliance are not just best practices—they are essential pillars for mitigating risks, adhering to regulatory standards, and maintaining organizational integrity. This chapter provides a comprehensive guide to implementing model governance, ensuring compliance, and managing risks effectively. Through structured frameworks, practical examples, and actionable strategies, you'll learn how to establish robust AI governance in your organization.

6.1 Governance Framework

Why Model Governance Matters

Model governance ensures that AI systems align with organizational goals, adhere to ethical standards, and operate within legal boundaries. A well-structured governance framework creates accountability, enhances transparency, and reduces risks.

Enterprise Model Governance Structure

1. Key Stakeholders

Role	Responsibility	Example Tasks
Model Risk Officer	Overall governance	Policy approval, escalation management
Model Validators	Independent review	Technical validation, performance checks
Business Owners	Use case oversight	ROI monitoring, aligning AI with strategy
Data Scientists	Model development	Documentation, addressing issues
Risk Committee	Risk supervision	Quarterly reviews, risk tiering assessments

2. Governance Bodies

Organizational Structure:

```
Board Level
└── AI Ethics Committee
├── Model Risk Committee
│ ├── Model Review Board
│ └── Technical Committee
└── Business Committee
├── Use Case Review
└── Value Assessment
```

This structure ensures that technical, ethical, and business considerations are integrated into the governance process.

6.2 Model Risk Management

Why Risk Management is Essential

AI models inherently involve risks, from technical errors to regulatory violations. A robust risk management framework helps identify, assess, and mitigate these risks to safeguard the organization's operations and reputation.

Risk Assessment Framework

1. Risk Categories

Category	Description	Examples	Mitigation
Technical Risk	Errors in model output	Poor accuracy, overfitting	Comprehensive validation
Business Risk	Negative business impact	Revenue loss, inefficiency	Performance monitoring
Regulatory Risk	Breach of regulations	GDPR non-compliance	Regular audits
Reputational Risk	Damage to public trust	Bias, unfair decisions	Ethical reviews

2. Risk Tiering

Risk Tier	Example Models	Characteristics
Tier 1 (High Risk)	Credit decisioning, trading algorithms, healthcare diagnostics	Critical decisions, high stakes
Tier 2 (Medium Risk)	Customer segmentation, pricing models, marketing optimization	Moderate impact, business-facing
Tier 3 (Low Risk)	Reporting automation, internal analytics, data visualization	Internal use, lower stakes

6.3 Documentation Requirements

Why Documentation is Critical

Comprehensive documentation provides transparency, ensures reproducibility, and supports compliance. It also acts as a communication bridge between technical teams, business stakeholders, and regulators.

Model Documentation

1. Model Cards

Model cards standardize the documentation process for AI systems.

Required Sections:

- **Model Overview:** Purpose, scope, and objectives.

- **Development Details:** Data sources, feature engineering, and algorithms.
- **Performance Metrics:** Accuracy, bias metrics, and business KPIs.
- **Risk Assessment:** Known limitations, edge cases, and mitigation plans.
- **Operational Details:** Deployment methods, monitoring plans, and maintenance schedules.

2. Version Control

Document	Update Frequency	Approver	Storage
Model Card	Each release	MRM Team	Model Registry
Technical Specifications	Major changes	Tech Lead	Git Repository
User Guide	Quarterly	Business Owner	SharePoint
Runbooks	As needed	Ops Team	Wiki

6.4 Compliance Requirements

Why Compliance is Non-Negotiable

Compliance ensures that AI systems operate within legal and ethical boundaries, protecting the organization from fines, legal action, and reputational damage.

Regulatory Framework

1. Common Regulations

Industry	Regulations
Financial Services	SR 11-7 (Fed), GDPR, CCPA
Healthcare	HIPAA, FDA regulations, HITECH Act
General	Data privacy laws, industry standards, internal policies

2. Compliance Checklist

Phase	Checklist Items
Pre-deployment	Data privacy assessment, model validation, risk assessment, ethics review, security audit
Post-deployment	Performance monitoring, audit logs, incident reports, documentation updates

6.5 Validation Process

Model Validation Framework

1. Validation Steps

1. **Conceptual Soundness:**
   - Review business logic and model assumptions.
   - Assess algorithm appropriateness.
2. **Technical Review:**
   - Conduct code reviews and performance testing.
   - Validate model implementation.
3. **Outcome Analysis:**
   - Verify results and benchmark comparisons.
   - Assess business impact.
4. **Ongoing Monitoring:**
   - Track performance, detect drift, and address issues promptly.

2. Validation Schedule

Model Tier	Initial Validation	Revalidation	Monitoring
Tier 1	4 weeks	6 months	Daily
Tier 2	2 weeks	Annual	Weekly
Tier 3	1 week	18 months	Monthly

6.6 Audit Management

Why Audits Matter

Audits ensure compliance, identify gaps, and reinforce accountability. They provide external validation of an organization's AI practices.

Audit Preparation

1. Audit Documentation

Document	Content
Model Inventory	List of production models, risk classifications, performance history
Validation Reports	Initial validation, periodic reviews, issue resolutions
Compliance Records	Regulatory checks, policy adherence, incident reports
Change Management	Version history, approvals, impact assessments

2. Audit Timeline

Phase	Activities
Pre-audit (4 weeks)	Document collection, self-assessment, gap analysis
During audit (2 weeks)	Presentation sessions, document review, Q&A
Post-audit (2 weeks)	Findings review, action plans, implementation

6.7 Issue Management

Response Procedures

1. Issue Classification

Severity	Description	Response Time	Example
Critical	Business impact	2 hours	Model failure
High	Performance issues	24 hours	Accuracy drop
Medium	Non-critical	1 week	Documentation gaps
Low	Minor updates	1 month	Version updates

2. Resolution Process

1. **Detection:** Identify and assess the issue.
2. **Investigation:** Analyze root cause and explore solutions.
3. **Resolution:** Implement fixes and validate outcomes.
4. **Prevention:** Update processes, refine controls, and conduct training.

6.8 Training and Awareness

Training Program

Audience	Topics	Frequency
Data Scientists	Model governance	Quarterly
Business Users	Model usage	Semi-annual
Risk Team	Risk assessment	Monthly
Executives	Overview	Annual

Training Materials

- Policy documents
- Process guides
- Case studies
- Best practices
- Compliance updates

Chapter Summary

- Establish governance structures with clear roles and responsibilities.
- Implement comprehensive risk management frameworks.
- Maintain detailed documentation and version control.
- Ensure compliance with industry standards and regulations.
- Conduct regular validations and audits.
- Manage issues effectively through structured processes.
- Provide ongoing training and awareness programs.

By following these practices, organizations can achieve sustainable, compliant, and ethical AI operations, ensuring both business success and public trust.

Chapter 7: AI Ethics and Responsible AI Implementation

Implementing ethical AI goes beyond theoretical principles—it requires actionable frameworks, practical tools, and clear processes to ensure responsible development and deployment. In an era where AI decisions affect individuals, businesses, and societies, embedding ethical considerations into every stage of AI development is crucial. This chapter equips you with the knowledge to operationalize AI ethics, focusing on fairness, transparency, privacy, accountability, and incident management in enterprise environments.

7.1 Ethical Framework Implementation

Why Ethical Frameworks Matter

Ethical frameworks ensure that AI systems align with organizational values, respect societal norms, and adhere to legal and regulatory standards. A well-designed ethical framework helps organizations minimize risks, build trust, and maximize the positive impact of AI technologies.

Enterprise Ethics Structure

1. Key Stakeholders and Responsibilities

Organizational Structure:

```
Ethics Board
├── Executive Sponsor
│ - Final approval authority
│ - Resource allocation
│
├── Ethics Committee
│ - Policy development
```

│ - Case review

│ - Guidelines updates

│

├── Technical Teams

│ - Implementation

│ - Testing

│ - Monitoring

│

└── Business Units

- Use case assessment

- Impact evaluation

- Feedback collection

This structure ensures collaboration between technical, ethical, and business perspectives, fostering a holistic approach to AI governance.

2. Review Process

Stage	Reviewers	Deliverables	Timeline
Initial Assessment	Business + Ethics	Impact Report	Week 1
Technical Review	ML Team + Ethics	Technical Analysis	Week 2
Stakeholder Review	All Parties	Final Approval	Week 3

This staged review process ensures that AI projects are ethically sound and aligned with organizational goals before deployment.

7.2 Fairness Assessment

Why Fairness Matters

AI systems often reflect the biases present in their training data or underlying algorithms. Ensuring fairness in AI decisions is critical to avoid perpetuating or amplifying systemic inequalities.

Practical Fairness Framework

1. Bias Detection Process

1. **Data Analysis:**
    - Evaluate demographic distribution.
    - Identify historical biases in the dataset.
    - Ensure adequate representation across all groups.
2. **Model Evaluation:**
    - Compare performance metrics across demographic groups.
    - Calculate disparity metrics to identify potential inequities.
    - Assess the real-world impact of model predictions.
3. **Mitigation:**
    - Rebalance datasets to improve representation.
    - Adjust algorithms to minimize bias.
    - Apply post-processing techniques to correct disparities in outcomes.

2. Key Metrics for Fairness

Metric	**Description**	**Target**	**Action if Missed**
Demographic Parity	Equal prediction rates	$\pm 5\%$	Data rebalancing
Equal Opportunity	Equal true positive rates	$\pm 3\%$	Model tuning
Disparate Impact	Ratio of favorable outcomes	>0.8	Process review

Real-World Example: Loan Approval System

Fairness Assessment Checklist

1. **Data Review:**
    - Analyze applicant demographics for representation.
    - Examine historical approval rates for potential biases.
    - Identify and address proxy variables that may introduce

unintended bias.

2. **Model Analysis:**
    - Compare approval rates across demographic groups.
    - Measure impact ratios to identify significant disparities.
    - Review edge cases for fairness issues.
3. **Documentation:**
    - Record findings and decisions in the assessment process.
    - Document changes made to address fairness concerns.
    - Track updates to datasets and models over time.

7.3 Transparency and Explainability

Why Transparency Matters

Transparency fosters trust by making AI systems understandable to users, regulators, and stakeholders. Explainability ensures that decisions made by AI systems can be justified and evaluated.

Implementation Framework

1. Documentation Requirements

Section	Content
Business Purpose	Use case description, intended users, and expected impact.
Technical Details	Algorithm rationale, feature importance, and limitations.
Decision Process	Key factors influencing decisions, weightings, and override procedures.

2. Explanation Methods by Use Case

Use Case	Method	Audience	Format
Credit Decision	LIME/SHAP	Customers	Factor list
Medical Diagnosis	Decision Trees	Doctors	Visual path
Fraud Detection	Feature Importance	Analysts	Dashboard

Practical Implementation

Explanation Framework:

```
Global Explanations
├── Model-level insights
│ - Feature importance
│ - Decision boundaries
│ - Overall patterns
│
Local Explanations
├── Instance-level details
│ - Individual predictions
│ - Factor contribution
│ - Counterfactuals
│
User Interface
└── Presentation layer
- Visualization
- Plain language
- Interactive elements
```

This structured approach ensures that AI systems provide both high-level insights and granular details tailored to different audiences.

7.4 Privacy Protection

Why Privacy is Essential

Protecting user privacy is a foundational ethical principle in AI. Data breaches, unauthorized use, and lack of transparency can erode trust and lead to regulatory penalties.

Privacy Implementation Framework

1. Data Protection Measures

Technical Controls:

- Encrypt data during transit and at rest.
- Implement strict access controls and permissions.
- Minimize data collection to only what is necessary.
- Anonymize data to protect individual identities.

Process Controls:

- Establish protocols for access requests.
- Define retention periods and ensure timely data deletion.
- Maintain detailed audit trails for all data interactions.

2. Privacy Impact Assessment

Component	Consideration	Action Items
Data Collection	Necessity	Minimize scope
Data Storage	Security	Encrypt sensitive fields
Data Usage	Purpose limitation	Document access
Data Sharing	Agreements	Review procedures

Real-World Example: Healthcare AI System

1. **Data Handling:**
    - Identify and protect personal health information (PHI).
    - De-identify datasets to ensure compliance.
    - Limit access to authorized personnel.
2. **System Design:**
    - Embed privacy by design into the system architecture.

- Implement advanced security measures to prevent breaches.
- Enable audit capabilities to track data usage.

3. **Compliance:**
    - Ensure adherence to HIPAA, GDPR, or equivalent regulations.
    - Establish robust consent management mechanisms.
    - Define clear procedures for breach management.

7.5 Accountability Framework

Practical Implementation

1. Responsibility Matrix

Role	Accountability	Tasks	Documentation
Model Owner	Overall success	Approval, monitoring	Quarterly review reports
Data Scientist	Technical implementation	Development, testing	Technical documentation
Business User	Use case compliance	Feedback, adjustments	Usage reports
Ethics Officer	Ethical oversight	Reviews, escalations	Assessment reports

2. Review Process

Frequency	Activities
Monthly	Performance metrics, bias monitoring, incident review
Quarterly	Impact assessments, policy compliance, stakeholder feedback
Annual	Comprehensive audits, framework updates, training refresh

7.6 Incident Response

Response Framework

Type	Description	Response Time	Example
Bias Incident	Unfair outcomes	24 hours	Demographic disparity
Privacy Breach	Data exposure	2 hours	Unauthorized access
Ethics Violation	Policy breach	48 hours	Misuse of system

Incident Response Flow:

1. **Detection:** Identify issue, assess impact, notify stakeholders.
2. **Investigation:** Conduct root cause analysis, develop solutions.
3. **Resolution:** Implement fixes, validate improvements, document actions.
4. **Prevention:** Update processes, provide training, enhance controls.

7.7 Training and Awareness

Audience	Topics	Frequency
Developers	Technical ethics	Quarterly
Business Users	Responsible use	Semi-annual
Leadership	Ethical strategy	Annual

Training Materials

- Ethics principles and compliance guidelines.
- Case studies and hands-on exercises.
- Tool-specific training and assessments.

Chapter Summary

- Build an ethical framework tailored to enterprise needs.
- Conduct fairness assessments to prevent biased outcomes.
- Ensure transparency and explainability for diverse audiences.
- Protect user privacy through robust technical and procedural controls.
- Define accountability roles with regular reviews.
- Develop an effective incident response strategy.
- Provide continuous training to embed ethics into organizational

culture.

This chapter equips enterprises with actionable strategies to implement AI ethics, ensuring that AI systems are both effective and aligned with organizational and societal values.

Chapter 8: End-to-End AI Project Case Study – Customer Churn Prevention System

This chapter presents a comprehensive case study on implementing a **Customer Churn Prevention System** for *GlobalTech Solutions*, a leading B2B SaaS company. Through this example, we'll walk through the end-to-end process of designing, deploying, and monitoring an AI solution while highlighting the practical application of concepts covered in earlier chapters.

8.1 Project Overview

Business Context

Company Profile:

- **Industry:** Enterprise Software
- **Revenue:** $500M annually
- **Customers:** 2,000+ enterprise clients
- **Problem:** 15% annual customer churn rate
- **Cost:** Average $250,000 per lost customer

The high churn rate was directly impacting *GlobalTech Solutions*' bottom line. Addressing this challenge became a top priority for the company's leadership.

Project Charter

Project	**Enterprise Customer Churn Prevention System**
Duration	6 months
Budget	$1.2M
Team Size	8 full-time members
Expected ROI	$5M annually

Key Stakeholders

Role	Department	Responsibility
Project Sponsor	C-Suite	Executive oversight
Product Owner	Customer Success	Business requirements
Data Science Lead	Analytics	Technical delivery
ML Engineer	Engineering	Implementation
Data Engineer	Data	Data pipeline
Risk Officer	Compliance	Governance
Ethics Officer	Legal	Ethical oversight
Business Analyst	Customer Success	Requirements gathering

8.2 Project Implementation

Phase 1: Data Strategy and Collection

1. Data Sources Inventory

System	Data
Salesforce (CRM):	Customer demographics, contract details, account history
Product Analytics:	Usage patterns, feature adoption, user engagement
Support System:	Ticket history, response times, resolution rates
Billing System:	Payment history, contract value, upgrades/downgrades

2. Data Quality Assessment

Source	Completeness	Accuracy	Freshness
CRM	95%	98%	Real-time
Analytics	92%	97%	Hourly
Support	98%	99%	Real-time
Billing	100%	100%	Daily

Phase 2: Feature Engineering

1. Feature Categories

Category	Key Metrics
Usage Metrics:	Daily active users, feature adoption rate, session duration
Support Metrics:	Ticket volume, resolution time, satisfaction scores
Financial Metrics:	Payment delays, contract changes, service upgrades
Engagement Metrics:	Response rates, meeting attendance, product feedback

2. Feature Store Design

Architecture:

```
├── Raw Features
│   ├── Real-time features
│   └── Batch features
├── Derived Features
│   ├── Aggregations
│   └── Transformations
└── Feature Sets
├── Training set
└── Prediction set
```

Phase 3: Model Development

1. Model Selection Process

Evaluation Criteria	Target/Requirement
Performance:	AUC-ROC > 0.85, Precision > 0.80, Recall > 0.75
Operational:	Inference time < 100ms, Update frequency: Daily
Business:	Interpretability required, real-time predictions

2. Model Architecture

Final Solution:

├── Primary Model

│ - XGBoost Classifier

│ - 100 features

│ - Daily retraining

├── Backup Model

│ - Random Forest

│ - Weekly updates

└── Business Rules

- Override conditions

- Manual reviews

Phase 4: Deployment Architecture

1. Production Environment

Infrastructure Design:

├── Data Pipeline (Airflow)

│ ├── Data collection

│ ├── Feature computation

│ └── Quality checks

│

├── Model Service (Kubernetes)

│ ├── Primary pod

│ ├── Backup pod

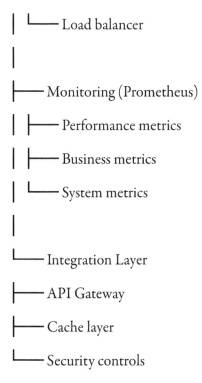

```
│ └── Load balancer
│
├── Monitoring (Prometheus)
│ ├── Performance metrics
│ ├── Business metrics
│ └── System metrics
│
└── Integration Layer
├── API Gateway
├── Cache layer
└── Security controls
```

2. Deployment Schedule

Week	Activity
Week 1	System integration, performance testing, UAT
Week 2	Pilot deployment (10% traffic), feedback collection
Week 3	Gradual rollout, performance optimization
Week 4	Full production, final validation, documentation

Phase 5: Monitoring and Maintenance

1. Monitoring Dashboard

Category	Metrics
Model Performance:	Prediction accuracy, response time, feature drift
Business Impact:	Churn reduction, revenue saved, customer satisfaction
System Health:	Resource usage, error rates, data quality

2. Maintenance Schedule

Activity	Frequency	Owner	Deliverable
Performance Review	Daily	ML Engineer	Status report
Business Review	Weekly	Product Owner	Impact report
Model Retraining	Monthly	Data Scientist	Updated model
Full Audit	Quarterly	Risk Officer	Audit report

Phase 6: Governance and Ethics

1. Governance Framework

Documentation	Content
Model Card	Model purpose, performance metrics, limitations
Risk Assessment	Technical risks, business risks, mitigation plans
Compliance Review	Privacy impact, fairness assessment, ethical guidelines

2. Ethics Checklist

Category	Checklist Items
Fairness:	Equal performance across segments, regular bias checks
Transparency:	Decision explanations, appeal process, documentation
Privacy:	Data minimization, access controls, retention policies

8.3 Project Results

Business Impact

Metric	Result
Churn Reduction	35%
Revenue Saved	$8.5M
ROI	708%
Customer Satisfaction	+15%

Technical Metrics

Metric	Value
AUC-ROC	0.87
Precision	0.83
Recall	0.79
Inference Time	85ms

Lessons Learned

1. **Success Factors:**
    - Strong stakeholder engagement.
    - Robust monitoring systems.
    - Clear governance framework.
2. **Challenges Faced:**
    - Data integration complexities.
    - Iterative feature engineering.
    - Production scaling issues.
3. **Best Practices Identified:**
    - Start with an MVP approach.
    - Prioritize robust monitoring.
    - Maintain thorough documentation.

Chapter Summary

This case study provided a practical, step-by-step guide for implementing an AI-powered customer churn prevention system. Key takeaways include:

- **End-to-End Implementation:** From data strategy to deployment.
- **Practical Considerations:** Addressing real-world constraints.
- **Measurable Outcomes:** Demonstrating ROI and business impact.
- **Lessons Learned:** Identifying best practices for future projects.

By following these strategies, organizations can successfully implement AI systems that deliver measurable business value while adhering to ethical and operational standards.

Chapter 9: End-to-End AI Project Case Study – Industrial Predictive Maintenance System

This chapter explores the implementation of an AI-powered **Predictive Maintenance System** at *ManufactureTech Industries*, a large manufacturing company operating multiple factories. By leveraging AI and IoT technologies, this project showcases how predictive analytics can optimize maintenance schedules, reduce unplanned downtime, and extend the lifecycle of industrial equipment. This case study offers a comprehensive walkthrough of the project lifecycle, from infrastructure setup to measurable results, emphasizing practical applications of AI in industrial settings.

9.1 Project Overview

Business Context

Company Profile:

- **Industry:** Manufacturing (Industrial Equipment)
- **Revenue:** $2B annually
- **Facilities:** 5 manufacturing plants
- **Problem:** $50M annual maintenance costs, 12% unplanned downtime
- **Impact:** Each hour of downtime costs $150,000

The high cost of unplanned downtime and maintenance inefficiencies drove *ManufactureTech Industries* to invest in an AI-driven predictive maintenance system to monitor equipment health, prevent failures, and reduce operating expenses.

Project Charter

Project	**AI-Powered Predictive Maintenance System**
Duration	9 months
Budget	$2.5M
Team Size	12 full-time members
Expected ROI	$15M annually

ROI Drivers:

- Reduction in unplanned downtime
- Optimization of maintenance schedules
- Extension of equipment lifespan

Key Stakeholders

Role	Department	Responsibility
Plant Manager	Operations	Executive sponsor
Maintenance Head	Engineering	Technical requirements
Data Science Lead	Analytics	Model development
IoT Engineer	Engineering	Sensor integration
Data Engineer	IT	Data pipeline
Safety Officer	HSE	Safety compliance
Operations Manager	Production	Business requirements
Quality Manager	Quality	Standards compliance

9.2 Project Implementation

Phase 1: Infrastructure and Data Collection

1. Sensor Infrastructure

Key sensors were strategically placed to monitor critical equipment parameters:

Sensor Type	Placement	Specifications
Vibration Sensors	Critical components	1000 Hz, 0.1g resolution
Temperature Sensors	Key heat points	1 Hz, ±0.5°C accuracy
Pressure Sensors	Hydraulic systems	10 Hz, 0–1000 psi range
Power Consumption	All equipment	1 Hz, ±1% accuracy

2. Data Architecture

The infrastructure supported real-time and batch processing, with a multi-layered architecture:

Data Flow:

```
Edge Devices
├── Local Processing
│   ├── Data filtering
│   ├── Aggregation
│   └── Compression
│
Cloud Storage
├── Raw data lake
├── Processed warehouse
└── Feature store
Real-time Stream
├── Apache Kafka
├── Redis Cache
└── Time-series DB
```

Phase 2: Data Processing and Feature Engineering

1. Data Types and Sources

Category	Source	Update Frequency	Volume
Sensor Data	IoT devices	Real-time	2TB/day
Maintenance Logs	CMMS	Daily	50MB/day
Equipment Specs	Asset DB	Monthly	1GB
Operational Data	SCADA	Real-time	500GB/day

2. Feature Development

Engineered features enhanced predictive accuracy:

Feature Type	Examples
Time-Domain Features	Rolling averages, peak-to-peak values, trend indicators
Frequency-Domain Features	FFT components, harmonic analysis, frequency bands
Contextual Features	Equipment age, maintenance history, environmental factors
Derived Indicators	Health scores, risk metrics, efficiency ratios

Phase 3: Model Development

1. Model Architecture

A multi-model system was designed to address diverse maintenance challenges:

```
├── Anomaly Detection
│   ├── Isolation Forest
│   └── AutoEncoder
│
├── Failure Prediction
│   ├── LSTM Network
│   └── Random Forest
│
```

```
│
├── Remaining Life Estimation
│ ├── Survival Analysis
│ └── Regression Models
│
└── Maintenance Optimization
├── Reinforcement Learning
└── Decision Trees
```

2. Model Training Strategy

Stage	Key Activities
Historical Training	2 years of historical data, known failure cases, maintenance records
Online Learning	Daily updates, feedback incorporation, model adaptation
Validation	Cross-validation, out-of-time validation, expert review

Phase 4: Production Deployment

1. System Architecture

The production environment ensured scalability, reliability, and integration:

```
Edge Layer
├── Local Processing Units
│ ├── Data collection
│ ├── Initial processing
│ └── Alert generation
│
```

```
Cloud Layer
├── Main Processing
│   ├── Model inference
│   ├── Deep analysis
│   └── Optimization
│
Integration Layer
├── CMMS Integration
├── SCADA Integration
└── ERP Integration
User Interface Layer
├── Web Dashboard
├── Mobile App
└── Alert System
```

Phase 5: Monitoring and Optimization

1. Key Metrics Dashboard

Category	Metrics
Technical Metrics	Model accuracy, false alarm rate, prediction lead time
Business Metrics	Downtime reduction, maintenance savings, labor efficiency
System Health	Sensor status, data quality, processing lag

2. Continuous Improvement Process

Step	Key Activities
Performance Analysis	Review accuracy, analyze false alarms, evaluate misses
System Optimization	Retrain models, tune parameters, adjust thresholds
Process Improvement	Update workflows, refine documentation, enhance training

Phase 6: Safety and Compliance

1. Safety Framework

Safety Protocols:

- Redundant sensors, failsafe modes, manual overrides, backup systems.

Compliance Checks:

- Industry standards, safety regulations, environmental rules.

9.3 Project Results

Business Impact

Metric	Result
Unplanned Downtime	Reduced by 45%
Maintenance Costs	Reduced by 30%
Equipment Lifespan	Increased by 25%
ROI	$12M achieved

Technical Achievements

Metric	Value
Failure Prediction Accuracy	92%
False Alarm Rate	<5%
Prediction Lead Time	2–4 weeks
System Availability	99.99%

Lessons Learned

1. **Critical Success Factors:**
    - High-quality sensors and strategic placement.
    - Cross-functional collaboration.
    - Robust validation and monitoring processes.
2. **Key Challenges:**
    - Managing sensor reliability.
    - Integration with legacy systems.
    - Mitigating alert fatigue.
3. **Best Practices:**
    - Start with critical equipment for rapid ROI.
    - Involve domain experts in validation.
    - Regularly update stakeholders on progress.

Chapter Summary

This case study highlights the real-world application of AI in industrial predictive maintenance, offering a detailed roadmap for implementation. Key takeaways include:

- **Multi-Layered Technical Solutions** that address diverse challenges.
- **Safety-Critical Considerations** for compliance and operational reliability.
- **Measurable Business Impact** in terms of downtime reduction and cost savings.

By following these strategies, organizations can leverage AI to drive efficiency, improve safety, and achieve significant financial gains.

Chapter 10: End-to-End AI Project Case Study – Clinical Decision Support System

This chapter delves into the implementation of an **AI-powered Clinical Decision Support System (CDSS)** at *MetroHealth Network*, a large healthcare organization operating multiple hospitals and clinics. The project highlights the complexities of deploying AI in regulated environments while demonstrating its transformative impact on clinical workflows, patient outcomes, and operational efficiency.

10.1 Project Overview

Business Context

Organization Profile:

Organizational Scope	Current Challenges
5 hospitals, 30 clinics	12% diagnostic revision rate
2,000+ beds	8% medication error rate
15,000 staff members	24-hour average test analysis time
2M+ patient visits annually	$30M annual cost from preventable complications

Healthcare systems like *MetroHealth Network* face significant challenges in delivering timely, accurate, and error-free care. Diagnostic revisions, medication errors, and delays in test result analysis lead to preventable complications and financial losses.

Project Charter

Project	**AI-Enhanced Clinical Decision Support System**
Duration	12 months
Budget	$4.5M
Team Size	15 full-time members
Expected Outcomes	- 30% reduction in diagnostic revisions - 50% reduction in medication errors - 75% faster test result analysis - $15M annual savings

Key Stakeholders

Role	Department	Responsibility
Chief Medical Officer	Executive	Executive sponsor
Clinical Director	Medical	Clinical requirements
Data Science Lead	Analytics	AI development
CMIO	Informatics	System integration
Privacy Officer	Legal	HIPAA compliance
IT Security	InfoSec	Security compliance
Quality Manager	Quality	Standards compliance
Department Heads	Various	Specialist input

10.2 Regulatory Compliance Framework

Healthcare Compliance Requirements

1. Regulatory Standards

Regulation	Key Focus Areas
HIPAA	Privacy Rule, Security Rule, Breach Notification
FDA Requirements	SaMD validation, risk classification
Joint Commission	Patient safety, quality metrics, documentation
State Regulations	Data protection, licensing, reporting

2. Documentation Requirements

Document Type	Purpose	Update Frequency	Approver
Clinical Validation	FDA Compliance	Initial + Major Changes	Medical Director
Privacy Impact	HIPAA Compliance	Quarterly	Privacy Officer
Security Assessment	InfoSec Requirements	Semi-annual	CISO
Clinical Protocols	Operating Procedures	Monthly	Clinical Director

10.3 Project Implementation

Phase 1: Clinical Data Integration

1. Data Sources

Source	Key Data Types
Electronic Health Records (EHR):	Patient demographics, medical history, lab results, medications, clinical notes, imaging reports
Clinical Systems:	Laboratory Information Systems (LIS), Radiology PACS, Pharmacy Systems, Vital Signs Monitors
External Data:	Claims data, research databases, drug databases, clinical guidelines

2. Data Integration Architecture

Healthcare Data Pipeline:

```
Source Systems
├── HL7 Interfaces
├── FHIR API
└── Direct Database
Integration Layer
├── Data Transformation
```

```
│ ├── SNOMED CT mapping
│ ├── ICD-10 coding
│ └── LOINC standardization
│
├── Quality Controls
│ ├── Completeness checks
│ ├── Consistency validation
│ └── Standard compliance
│
Data Warehouse
├── Clinical data mart
├── Research database
└── Audit logs
```

Phase 2: Clinical Feature Engineering

1. Feature Categories

Feature Type	Examples
Patient Characteristics	Demographics, vital trends, family history
Clinical Indicators	Lab values, symptom patterns, disease progression
Treatment Features	Medication history, procedure outcomes
Contextual Features	Care setting, provider specialty, time patterns

2. Feature Validation Process

Validation Area	Key Activities
Medical Review	Evaluate clinical relevance, evidence basis, and safety implications
Technical Validation	Assess data quality, feature stability, and population coverage
Regulatory Review	Ensure HIPAA compliance, FDA requirements, and proper documentation

Phase 3: Model Development

1. Clinical Model Architecture

Multi-Module System:

```
Risk Assessment
├── Admission Risk
├── Complication Risk
└── Mortality Risk
Diagnostic Support
├── Primary Diagnosis
├── Differential Diagnosis
└── Rare Disease Detection
Treatment Optimization
├── Medication Selection
├── Dosage Optimization
└── Interaction Checking
Resource Optimization
├── Length of Stay
```

├── Resource Utilization

└── Capacity Planning

2. Validation Framework

Validation Area	Activities
Technical Validation	Cross-validation, subgroup analysis, performance metrics
Clinical Validation	Expert review, case studies, clinical trials
Safety Validation	Error analysis, edge cases, failure modes

Phase 4: Clinical Deployment

1. Implementation Strategy

Phase	Key Activities
Phase 1: Shadow Mode	Validate outputs, gather feedback, run alongside existing processes
Phase 2: Limited Release	Deploy in selected departments, monitor closely, iterate based on feedback
Phase 3: Full Deployment	Expand across all departments with ongoing monitoring and regular updates

2. Workflow Integration

Area	Key Integrations
EHR Integration	Order entry, clinical alerts, documentation
Workflow Integration	Care pathways, emergency protocols, clinical protocols
User Interface	Physician dashboards, nurse views, mobile access

Phase 5: Clinical Monitoring

1. Monitoring Framework

Category	Metrics
Clinical Metrics	Diagnostic accuracy, treatment outcomes, length of stay
Technical Metrics	Model performance, response time, system uptime
Safety Metrics	Adverse events, near-misses, recovery times

2. Quality Assurance

Frequency	Activities
Daily	Check system health, data quality, alert volumes
Weekly	Analyze performance trends, user feedback
Monthly	Conduct compliance audits, review outcomes

10.4 Clinical Results

Clinical Impact

Metric	Result
Diagnostic Accuracy	Improved by 35%
Medication Errors	Reduced by 55%
Test Analysis Time	Reduced by 80%
Cost Savings	$18M annually

Patient Outcomes

Metric	Result
Length of Stay	Reduced by 2.5 days on average
Complications	Reduced by 40%
Readmissions	Reduced by 30%
Patient Satisfaction	Increased by 25%

Lessons Learned

1. **Success Factors:**
    - Clinical engagement and phased implementation.
    - Rigorous validation processes.
    - Continuous monitoring and regular updates.
2. **Challenges Overcome:**

  - Achieving clinical acceptance and workflow integration.
  - Managing data standardization and regulatory compliance.
3. **Best Practices:**
  - Focus on high-impact areas first.
  - Involve clinicians from the outset.
  - Maintain transparency and detailed documentation.

Chapter Summary

This case study demonstrates the application of AI in healthcare to improve diagnostic accuracy, reduce medication errors, and enhance patient outcomes. Key takeaways include:

- **Rigorous Compliance:** Navigating HIPAA, FDA, and Joint Commission standards.
- **Clinical Validation:** Ensuring AI aligns with medical best practices.
- **Patient-Centric Outcomes:** Achieving measurable improvements in care delivery.

This example sets a benchmark for deploying AI in healthcare with a focus on ethics, safety, and clinical impact.

Chapter 11: End-to-End AI Project Case Study – Real-Time Fraud Detection System

This case study details the implementation of an AI-powered Fraud Detection System at *GlobalBank Financial*, a multinational bank with operations in retail, commercial, and investment banking. The project highlights the complexities of implementing AI in highly regulated financial environments, showcasing how advanced systems can mitigate fraud, streamline operations, and enhance customer experience.

11.1 Project Overview

Business Context

Organization Profile: GlobalBank Financial

- **Operations in 25 countries**
- **50M+ retail customers**
- **2M+ business customers**
- **$5T+ annual transaction volume**
- **Current Challenges:**
    - $200M annual fraud losses
    - 500+ fraud analysts
    - 2,000+ false positives daily
    - 48-hour average fraud investigation time
    - 15% customer friction from false alerts

Project Charter

- **Project:** AI-Enhanced Fraud Detection System
- **Duration:** 15 months
- **Budget:** $8M
- **Team Size:** 20 full-time members
- **Expected Outcomes:**
    - 60% reduction in fraud losses

    - 80% reduction in false positives
    - 90% faster investigation time
    - Improved customer experience
- **ROI Target:** $120M annually

Key Stakeholders

Role	Department	Responsibility
Chief Risk Officer	Executive	Executive sponsor
Fraud Director	Risk	Define business requirements
Data Science Lead	Analytics	Develop AI models
InfoSec Head	Security	Ensure system security
Compliance Head	Legal	Oversee regulatory compliance
Operations Head	Operations	Integrate fraud processes
Customer Experience	Digital	Enhance customer journey
IT Architecture	Technology	System integration

11.2 Regulatory Framework

Financial Compliance Requirements

1. Regulatory Standards

- **Anti-Money Laundering (AML):**
    - Transaction monitoring
    - Customer due diligence
    - Regulatory reporting
- **Know Your Customer (KYC):**
    - Identity verification
    - Risk assessment
    - Enhanced due diligence
- **Payment Regulations:**
    - PSD2 compliance
    - SWIFT guidelines
    - Local regulations
- **Data Protection:**

- GDPR compliance
- CCPA requirements
- Banking secrecy laws

2. Audit Requirements

Area	Frequency	Documentation	Reviewer
Model Risk	Quarterly	Model validation	Risk Committee
AML Compliance	Monthly	SAR reports	Compliance Officer
Data Privacy	Semi-annual	DPIA	Data Protection Officer
System Security	Continuous	Penetration test results	CISO

11.3 Project Implementation

Phase 1: Data Architecture

1. Data Sources

Category	Details
Transaction Data:	Card transactions, online payments, ATM withdrawals
Account Activities:	Wire transfers, standing orders, direct debits
Customer Data:	Profile information, account history, device details
External Data:	Credit bureau reports, sanctions lists, fraud databases, device intelligence

2. Real-Time Data Processing

Stream Processing Architecture:

- **Data Ingestion**
    - Real-time Streams: Apache Kafka, Redis Cache, Event Hub
- **Processing Layer**

  - Stream Processing: Apache Flink, Feature Computation, Rule Engine
- **Storage Layer**
  - Hot Storage: Redis
  - Warm Storage: Cassandra
  - Cold Storage: Data Lake

Phase 2: Feature Engineering

1. Feature Categories

Feature Type	Examples
Transaction Features:	Amount patterns, frequency patterns, location patterns, time patterns
Derived Features:	Velocity checks, pattern deviations, risk scores, anomaly indicators
Customer Features:	Historical behavior, risk profiles, segment indicators
Network Features:	Connection patterns, entity relationships, risk propagation

2. Real-Time Feature Processing

- **Real-time Features:** Current transaction, recent history (24h), device signals
- **Near Real-time Features:** Daily aggregates, weekly patterns, network metrics
- **Batch Features:** Historical patterns, risk profiles, network analysis

Phase 3: Model Development

1. Multi-Layer Detection System

Detection Layers:

- **Rule Engine:** Regulatory rules, policy rules, threshold rules
- **ML Models:** Random Forest, XGBoost, Deep Learning

- **Network Analysis:** Graph Neural Networks, Link Analysis, Pattern Detection
- **Ensemble Layer:** Model combination, risk aggregation, decision logic

2. Model Training Strategy

Stage	Activities
Data Preparation:	Balanced sampling, synthetic data generation, cross-validation sets
Training Process:	Model-specific training, hyperparameter optimization, ensemble calibration
Validation:	Statistical validation, business validation, compliance review

Phase 4: Production Deployment

1. System Architecture

Layer	Components
Real-Time Layer:	Feature service, model service, decision engine
Investigation Layer:	Alert queuing, investigation tools, decision support
Integration Layer:	Banking systems, payment networks, external services

2. Alert Management

Risk Level	Response Action
Critical	Immediate block
High	Detailed review
Medium	Monitoring and alerts
Low	Allow with flags

11.4 Results and Impact

Business Impact

- **Fraud Losses:** Reduced by 65%
- **False Positives:** Reduced by 85%
- **Investigation Time:** Reduced by 92%

- **Customer Friction:** Reduced by 70%
- **ROI Achieved:** $150M annually

Technical Metrics

- **Transaction Processing:** <50ms
- **Model Accuracy:** 99.95%
- **System Uptime:** 99.999%
- **Alert Precision:** 85%

Lessons Learned

Aspect	Details
Success Factors:	Real-time capabilities, multi-layer approach, strong governance, team expertise, stakeholder alignment
Challenges Overcome:	Data quality, real-time performance, false positives, regulatory compliance, change management
Best Practices:	Start with high-risk areas, build in compliance, focus on real-time, maintain flexibility, regular updates

Chapter Summary

This case study illustrates:

- The successful application of real-time AI systems in financial fraud detection.
- A focus on regulatory compliance, ensuring adherence to legal and privacy standards.
- The benefits of a multi-layer detection system combining rules, machine learning, and network analysis.
- Measurable business and operational outcomes with reduced fraud losses and improved customer experience.

Chapter 12: End-to-End AI Project Case Study – Retail Demand Forecasting System

This case study explores the implementation of an AI-powered Demand Forecasting and Inventory Optimization System at *RetailMax*, a large retail chain operating both physical stores and e-commerce platforms. It demonstrates the intricacies of deploying AI in a multi-channel retail environment to address challenges such as excess inventory, stockouts, and markdown losses.

12.1 Project Overview

Business Context

Organization Profile: RetailMax

- **Retail Operations:**
    - 500 physical stores
    - E-commerce platform
    - 50,000 SKUs
    - $5B annual revenue

Current Challenges:

1. $200M excess inventory
2. 15% stockout rate
3. 30% markdown losses
4. 25 days average inventory
5. 60% forecast accuracy

Project Charter

- **Project:** AI-Enhanced Demand Forecasting System
- **Duration:** 12 months
- **Budget:** $6M
- **Team Size:** 18 full-time members

- **Expected Outcomes:**
  - Reduce excess inventory by 40%
  - Decrease stockouts by 60%
  - Improve forecast accuracy to 85%
  - Reduce markdown losses by 50%
- **ROI Target:** $100M annually

Key Stakeholders

Role	Department	Responsibility
Supply Chain VP	Operations	Executive sponsor
Merchandise Director	Buying	Define business requirements
Store Operations	Retail	Oversee store implementation
E-commerce Head	Digital	Online integration
Data Science Lead	Analytics	Develop AI models
IT Director	Technology	System integration
Finance Director	Finance	Budget oversight
Logistics Head	Supply Chain	Distribution planning

12.2 Solution Architecture

Data Integration Framework

1. Data Sources

Category	Details
Sales Data:	Store POS (transactions, product info, promotions), e-commerce platform (orders, browse patterns)
External Data:	Weather, local events, competitor info, economic indicators
Operational Data:	Inventory levels, supply chain details, staffing data, store layouts

2. Integration Architecture

Data Pipeline:

- **Source Systems:** Store systems, e-commerce platform, ERP system, external APIs
- **Integration Layer:**
    - **Data Lake:** Historical data, real-time feeds, external data
    - **Data Warehouse:** Cleaned data, aggregations, business rules
    - **Feature Store:** Store features, product features, time features

12.3 Project Implementation

Phase 1: Feature Engineering

1. Feature Categories

Feature Type	Examples
Historical Patterns:	Sales trends (daily/weekly/seasonal), special events
Product Features:	Category, price point, elasticity, substitutability
Location Features:	Store characteristics (size, demographics, competition)
External Features:	Weather, events, economic indicators, competitor actions

2. Feature Processing Pipeline

- **Data Cleaning:** Handle missing values, detect outliers, validate quality
- **Feature Creation:** Aggregations, rolling statistics, derived metrics
- **Feature Selection:** Correlation analysis, importance ranking, business validation

Phase 2: Model Development

1. Forecasting Architecture

Multi-Level Forecasting:

- **Store-Level Models:** Daily forecasts, weekly patterns, local events
- **Category-Level Models:** Seasonal trends, category interactions,

promotion effects

- **Chain-Level Models:** Overall trends, market conditions, strategic planning

Integration Layer:

- Model ensemble, reconciliation, business rules

2. Model Components

Type	Examples
Statistical Models:	SARIMA, exponential smoothing, Bayesian methods
Machine Learning:	XGBoost, LightGBM, neural networks
Deep Learning:	LSTM, transformers, attention models
Hybrid Approaches:	Model stacking, weighted ensembles, dynamic selection

Phase 3: Optimization Engine

1. Inventory Optimization

Component	Examples
Safety Stock:	Service level targets, demand uncertainty, cost constraints
Reorder Points:	Demand forecast, lead time, order constraints
Order Quantities:	Economic order quantity, storage constraints, transportation costs

2. Distribution Strategy

- **Allocation Rules:** Store priorities, service levels, cost optimization
- **Transfer Logic:** Inter-store transfers, DC optimization, route planning
- **Emergency Rules:** Stockout prevention, expedited shipping, alternative sourcing

Phase 4: Production Deployment

1. System Architecture

Layer	Components
Forecasting Engine:	Model services, feature services, integration APIs
Optimization Engine:	Inventory optimization, distribution planning, order management
User Interface:	Dashboard, alert system, report generator
Integration Layer:	ERP connection, store systems, e-commerce platform

2. Operational Workflow

Time	Activities
Morning:	Data refresh, forecast updates, priority alerts, order proposals
Day:	Real-time monitoring, exception handling, order adjustments
Evening:	Results analysis, next-day planning, report generation, system backup

Phase 5: Performance Monitoring

1. KPI Dashboard

Metric Type	Examples
Forecast Accuracy:	MAPE by category, bias metrics, hit rate, exception rate
Inventory Health:	Stock levels, turnover rate, service level, aging analysis
Financial Impact:	Inventory value, markdown loss, stockout cost, transportation cost

2. Continuous Improvement

Cycle	Activities
Daily:	Accuracy metrics, exception analysis, system health checks
Weekly:	Performance trends, pattern changes, model updates
Monthly:	Strategic reviews, resource planning, training needs

12.4 Results and Impact

Business Impact

- **Forecast Accuracy:** Improved to 88%
- **Excess Inventory:** Reduced by 45%
- **Stockout Rate:** Reduced to 5%
- **Markdown Losses:** Reduced by 55%
- **ROI Achieved:** $120M annually

Operational Improvements

- **Inventory Turns:** +40%
- **Working Capital:** -$150M
- **Labor Efficiency:** +25%
- **Customer Satisfaction:** +30%

Lessons Learned

Aspect	Details
Success Factors:	Data quality, stakeholder alignment, change management, continuous monitoring
Challenges Overcome:	Legacy system integration, data consistency, process change, user adoption

Chapter Summary

This case study highlights:

- Retail-specific AI implementation challenges and solutions.
- The integration of multi-channel data for demand forecasting.
- AI-driven inventory optimization processes.
- Tangible improvements in operational efficiency and financial outcomes.

Chapter 13: AI System Integration and Scale

Successfully integrating AI systems into enterprise environments and scaling them effectively presents unique challenges. This chapter provides practical approaches to integration, scaling, and optimization, based on real-world enterprise implementations.

13.1 Enterprise Integration Patterns

Legacy System Integration

1. Common Enterprise Systems

- **Core Systems:**
  - ERP Systems: SAP, Oracle, Microsoft Dynamics
  - CRM Platforms: Salesforce, Microsoft Dynamics, Oracle Siebel
  - Database Systems: Oracle, SQL Server, DB2
  - Custom Applications: Internal tools, department systems, legacy applications

2. Integration Methods

Method	Use Case	Pros	Cons
API Integration	Modern systems	Clean, standardized	API availability
Database Links	Direct data access	Fast, reliable	Security concerns
Message Queue	Async operations	Decoupled, scalable	Complex setup
File Transfer	Batch processing	Simple, universal	Latency issues

Integration Architecture

1. API Layer Design

- **API Gateway:**
  - **Authentication:** OAuth 2.0, API Keys, JWT Tokens
  - **Rate Limiting:** Per-user limits, service limits, quota management
  - **Request Routing:** Load balancing, service discovery, version control

    - **Monitoring:** Performance metrics, error tracking, usage analytics

2. Service Mesh Implementation

Component	Functionality
Control Plane:	Service registry, configuration, policy management
Data Plane:	Service discovery, load balancing, circuit breaking, observability
Security:	mTLS, authorization, rate limiting

13.2 Scaling Strategies

Infrastructure Scaling

1. Horizontal Scaling

- **Kubernetes Cluster:**
    - **Model Serving:** Pod autoscaling with CPU and memory thresholds
    - **Node Pools:** CPU optimized, GPU nodes, memory optimized
    - **Load Distribution:** Service mesh, ingress control, traffic splitting

2. Vertical Scaling

- **Resource Optimization:**
    - Compute resources: Base (4 cores), Max (16 cores), Burst (32 cores)
    - Memory: Base (16GB), Max (64GB), Swap disabled
    - GPU allocation: Training (4 GPUs), Inference (1 GPU), Shared enabled

Performance Optimization

1. Caching Strategy

- **Multi-Level Cache:**
    - **L1 (In-Memory Cache):** Redis Cluster for hot predictions, feature values, session data

- **L2 (Distributed Cache):** Prediction results, feature sets, model metadata
- **L3 (Edge Cache):** Static resources, common responses, configuration

2. Query Optimization

- **Database Optimization:**
  - Index strategy: Primary, secondary, composite indices
  - Query patterns: Prepared statements, connection pooling
  - Partitioning: Range, hash, list partitioning

13.3 Production Architecture

High Availability Design

1. System Architecture

Layer	Components
Load Balancer:	Primary (US-East), Secondary (US-West), SSL termination
Application Tier:	Auto-scaling groups, multi-AZ deployment, blue-green updates
Database Tier:	Primary cluster, read replicas, backup strategy

2. Failover Process

- **Disaster Recovery:**
  - Detection: 30 seconds
  - Failover time: 2 minutes
  - Data loss: <5 seconds
- **Recovery Steps:**
  - Health check failure
  - DNS failover
  - Cache warming
  - Service verification

Monitoring and Alerting

1. Monitoring Stack

- **Metrics Collection:** Prometheus (system, business, custom metrics)
- **Visualization:** Grafana (system, business, alert dashboards)
- **Log Management:** ELK Stack (log collection, analysis, retention)

2. Alert Framework

Priority	Description	Response Time
Critical Alerts (P1)	Service down, data loss	15 minutes
High Priority (P2)	Performance degradation	1 hour
Medium Priority (P3)	Warning thresholds, minor issues	4 hours

13.4 Cost Management

Resource Optimization

1. Infrastructure Costs

- **Cost Centers:**
  - Compute resources: VM instances, Kubernetes clusters, GPU instances
  - Storage resources: Object storage, block storage, database storage
  - Network resources: Data transfer, load balancers, VPN connections

2. Optimization Strategies

- **Cost Reduction Approaches:**
  - Resource scheduling: Auto-scaling, spot instances, reserved capacity
  - Storage optimization: Data lifecycle, compression, archival
  - Network optimization: CDN usage, caching, traffic routing

13.5 Best Practices

Implementation Guidelines

1. Integration Checklist

Stage	Activities
Pre-Integration:	System assessment, capacity planning, security review
During Integration:	Phased rollout, monitoring setup, backup procedures
Post-Integration:	Performance validation, security audit, user training

2. Maintenance Procedures

Frequency	Tasks
Daily Tasks:	Performance monitoring, error checking, backups
Weekly Tasks:	Capacity planning, performance tuning, updates
Monthly Tasks:	Full system review, cost optimization, compliance

Chapter Summary

This chapter covers:

- Integration patterns for legacy and modern enterprise systems.
- Scaling strategies for high-performance AI solutions.
- Optimization techniques for performance and cost management.
- Best practices for implementation, maintenance, and monitoring.

Chapter 14: AI System Security

Security in AI systems requires a comprehensive approach covering data, model, and infrastructure protection. This chapter details practical security implementations based on real-world enterprise deployments.

14.1 Security Framework

Enterprise Security Architecture

1. Security Layers

Defense-in-Depth Strategy:

- **Perimeter Security:**
    - Network Firewalls: Palo Alto Networks, Cisco ASA, Fortinet
- **Infrastructure Security:**
    - Cloud Security: AWS Security Groups, Azure NSG, GCP Firewall Rules
- **Application Security:**
    - Web Application Firewall (WAF): Cloudflare, AWS WAF, F5 Networks
- **Data Security:**
    - Encryption: At-rest, In-transit, In-use

2. Security Controls Matrix

Layer	Control Type	Implementation	Monitoring
Network	Access Control	Zero Trust	Real-time
Application	Authentication	MFA	Continuous
Data	Encryption	AES-256	Daily audit
Model	Protection	Adversarial defense	Ongoing

14.2 Threat Protection

Model Security

1. Model Protection Measures

Protection Framework:

- **Input Validation:**
    - Data sanitization, type checking, range validation, format verification
- **Attack Detection:**
    - Adversarial detection, pattern analysis, anomaly detection, input screening
- **Model Hardening:**
    - Adversarial training, attack simulation, defense optimization, robustness testing

2. Common Attack Vectors

Attack Type	Prevention/Defense
Model Extraction	Rate limiting, query monitoring, output randomization
Data Poisoning	Input validation, data verification, anomaly detection
Adversarial Attacks	Input preprocessing, model robustness, output verification

Data Security

1. Data Protection Framework

Data Security Layers:

Category	Subcategory	Description
Storage Security	Encryption Methods	AES-256 (at-rest), TLS 1.3 (in-transit), Homomorphic Encryption (in-use)
Access Control	Authentication	Multi-factor, Role-based, Context-based
Monitoring	Access Logging	User activity, system access, data movement

2. Privacy Protection

Privacy Controls:

- **Data Minimization:** Collection, storage, and usage limits
- **Anonymization:** Pseudonymization, k-anonymity, differential privacy
- **Access Management:** Need-to-know basis, time-limited access, purpose limitation

14.3 Security Operations

SOC Integration

1. Security Monitoring

Monitoring Framework:

- **Real-time Monitoring:**
  - SIEM Integration: Splunk, IBM QRadar, Microsoft Sentinel
  - Alert Management: Critical (15 min), High (1 hr), Medium (4 hr)
- **Response Procedures:**
  - Incident Types: Security breach, data leak, system compromise

2. Incident Response

Response Protocol:

- **Detection Phase:** Alert trigger, initial assessment, severity classification
- **Investigation Phase:** Log analysis, impact assessment, root cause analysis
- **Remediation Phase:** Threat containment, system recovery, control updates

Security Testing

1. Testing Framework

Security Testing Types:

- **Penetration Testing:** External scan, internal scan, vulnerability assessment
- **Application Testing:** SAST, DAST, IAST
- **Model Testing:** Input fuzzing, boundary testing, attack simulation

2. Compliance Testing

Compliance Checks:

Compliance Type	Standards/Requirements
Regulatory Compliance	SOC 2, ISO 27001, HIPAA, GDPR
Industry Compliance	PCI DSS, NIST, CIS Controls
Internal Compliance	Security policies, access policies, data handling

14.4 Security Infrastructure

Infrastructure Protection

1. Cloud Security

Cloud Security Controls:

- **Identity Management:** IAM configuration with role definitions, permission sets, and access policies
- **Network Security:** VPC setup with subnet isolation, security groups, and NACLs
- **Resource Protection:** Encryption, monitoring, and backup controls

2. Container Security

Container Protection:

- **Image Security:** Vulnerability scanning, image signing, registry security
- **Runtime Security:** Container isolation, resource limits, behavior monitoring
- **Orchestration Security:** Kubernetes security, secret management, network policies

14.5 Compliance and Audit

Compliance Framework

1. Compliance Requirements

Compliance Areas:

- **Data Protection:** Data classification, access controls, audit trails
- **Model Governance:** Model validation, bias detection, documentation
- **System Security:** Security controls, risk assessment, incident response

2. Audit Procedures

Audit Framework:

- **Regular Audits:** Daily monitoring, weekly reviews, monthly assessments, quarterly audits
- **Audit Areas:** Access controls, data protection, model security, system security
- **Documentation Requirements:** Audit logs, control evidence, policy compliance

Chapter Summary

This chapter covers:

- Security architecture for comprehensive protection.

- Threat protection mechanisms to safeguard AI systems.
- Security operations, including monitoring and incident response.
- Infrastructure security controls for cloud and containerized environments.
- Compliance management for regulatory adherence and audit preparation.

Chapter 15: Advanced AI Applications

Advanced AI applications require specialized architectures, tools, and implementation strategies. This chapter covers practical implementations of computer vision, NLP, and recommendation systems in enterprise environments.

15.1 Computer Vision Systems

Enterprise Vision Architecture

1. Vision Pipeline Components

Vision System Architecture:

- **Image Acquisition:**
  - Input Sources: Industrial cameras, security cameras, mobile devices, document scanners
- **Preprocessing Pipeline:**
  - Image Processing: Resizing (standardize to 640x640), normalization (0-1 scaling), real-time augmentation, quality enhancement
- **Model Pipeline:**
  - Detection Models: Primary (YOLOv8), backup (Faster R-CNN), specialized (Custom CNN)
- **Post-processing:**
  - Result Processing: NMS threshold (0.45), confidence filter (0.6), result aggregation

2. Implementation Use Cases

Industry	Application	Requirements	Key Metrics
Manufacturing	Quality Control	30fps, 4K	99.9% accuracy
Retail	Security	Real-time, 1080p	95% detection
Healthcare	Medical Imaging	High precision	99% specificity
Agriculture	Crop Analysis	Drone feed, 4K	90% coverage

Vision System Implementation

1. Production Architecture

Deployment Stack:

- **Edge Processing:**
  - Hardware: NVIDIA Jetson, Intel NCS2, Custom ASIC
- **Cloud Processing:**
  - GPU Clusters: V100 instances, A100 instances, load balancing
- **Storage System:**
  - Image Storage: Hot storage (7 days), warm storage (90 days), cold storage (archive)

2. Performance Optimization

Optimization Strategies:

- **Model Optimization:**
  - Techniques: Model quantization (INT8), pruning (30% reduction), knowledge distillation, TensorRT conversion
- **Pipeline Optimization:**
  - Methods: Batch processing, parallel inference, cache management, stream processing
- **Resource Management:**
  - Controls: GPU memory optimization, load distribution, resource scheduling

15.2 Natural Language Processing (NLP)

Enterprise NLP Architecture

1. NLP System Components

NLP Architecture:

- **Text Processing:**
    - Input Processing: Tokenization, cleaning, normalization, language detection
- **Model Pipeline:**
    - Model Stack: Base (BERT/RoBERTa), specialized (domain-tuned), task-specific (fine-tuned)
- **Output Processing:**
    - Post-processing: Result aggregation, confidence scoring, format conversion

2. Implementation Matrix

Use Case	**Components/Features**
Document Processing	OCR integration, layout analysis, content extraction, metadata generation
Sentiment Analysis	Multi-language support, real-time processing, aspect-based analysis, trend detection
Machine Translation	50+ languages, domain adaptation, quality estimation, terminology management

NLP Production Environment

1. System Architecture

Production Setup:

- **Processing Layer:**
    - Text Processing: Language workers, model workers, output workers
- **Model Layer:**
    - Model Services: Base models, fine-tuned models, specialized models
- **Integration Layer:**
    - API Services: REST endpoints, streaming service, batch processing

2. Scalability Framework

Scaling Strategy:

- **Horizontal Scaling:**
  - Configuration: Worker pools, load balancing, service discovery, auto-scaling
- **Resource Management:**
  - Allocation: CPU optimization, memory management, GPU utilization, cache strategy
- **Performance Monitoring:**
  - Metrics: Response time, throughput, error rates, resource usage

15.3 Recommendation Systems

Recommendation Architecture

1. System Components

Recommendation Stack:

- **Data Collection:**
  - User Data: Behavior tracking, profile data, preference data
- **Feature Processing:**
  - Feature Engineering: User features, item features, contextual features
- **Model Pipeline:**
  - Model Types: Collaborative filtering, content-based, hybrid models

2. Implementation Strategy

Production Implementation:

- **Real-time Processing:**
  - Components: Stream processing, feature computation, score

generation, ranking system

- **Batch Processing:**
  - Pipeline: Daily updates, model retraining, feature refresh, trend analysis
- **Serving Layer:**
  - Services: API endpoints, cache system, monitoring, A/B testing

Performance Optimization

1. Optimization Framework

Performance Tuning:

- **Response Time Targets:**
  - P95 < 100ms, P99 < 200ms, error rate < 0.1%
- **Resource Usage Limits:**
  - CPU: 70% max, memory: 80% max, network: 60% capacity
- **Cache Strategy:**
  - Hot items (Redis), warm items (Memcached), cold items (Database)

2. Scaling Strategy

Scale Management:

- **Load Distribution:**
  - Methods: Geographic distribution, service sharding, load balancing, traffic routing
- **Resource Allocation:**
  - Strategy: Dynamic provisioning, resource pooling, capacity planning, cost optimization
- **Monitoring System:**
  - Components: Performance metrics, business metrics, system health, alert system

15.4 Integration and Management

System Integration

1. Integration Framework

Enterprise Integration:

- **API Layer:**
  - Services: REST APIs, GraphQL, gRPC services, webhooks
- **Data Integration:**
  - Methods: ETL pipelines, stream processing, batch processing, real-time sync
- **Security Layer:**
  - Controls: Authentication, authorization, encryption, monitoring

2. Operational Management

Operations Framework:

- **Monitoring:**
  - Systems: Performance monitoring, error tracking, usage analytics, cost tracking
- **Maintenance:**
  - Schedule: Daily health checks, weekly updates, monthly review, quarterly planning
- **Documentation:**
  - Requirements: API documentation, system architecture, operational procedures, troubleshooting guides

Chapter Summary

This chapter covers:

- Vision systems implementation.
- NLP system architecture and applications.

- Recommendation systems in production.
- Integration strategies for enterprise environments.
- Operational management for AI systems.

Chapter 16: AI System Cost Optimization

Cost optimization in AI systems requires balancing performance requirements with resource efficiency. This chapter covers practical approaches to managing and optimizing costs in enterprise AI deployments.

16.1 Cost Analysis Framework

Cost Structure Analysis

1. Cost Categories

Enterprise AI Costs:

- **Infrastructure Costs:**
    - Compute Resources:
        - Training environments: Average $10K–50K/month
        - Production inference: Average $5K–25K/month
        - Development environments: Average $2K–10K/month
    - Storage Costs:
        - Raw data: $0.02–$0.05/GB
        - Processed data: $0.05–$0.10/GB
        - Model artifacts: $0.08–$0.15/GB
    - Network Costs:
        - Data Transfer:
            - Ingress: Often free
            - Egress: $0.08–$0.15/GB
            - Inter-region: $0.02–$0.05/GB

2. Cost Attribution Matrix

Component	Fixed Costs	Variable Costs	Optimization Potential
Training	Hardware lease	GPU usage	30–50%
Inference	Base infrastructure	Request volume	40–60%
Storage	Minimum retention	Data growth	20–40%

Resource Utilization Analysis

1. Usage Patterns

Resource Analysis:

- **Compute Usage:**
  - Peak hours: 9 AM–5 PM
  - Low usage: 11 PM–6 AM
  - Weekend baseline: 30%
  - Monthly spikes: End of month
- **Storage Growth:**
  - Raw data: 20% monthly
  - Processed data: 15% monthly
  - Archive data: 10% monthly
  - Model versions: 5% monthly
- **Network Traffic:**
  - Internal: 60%
  - External: 30%
  - Cross-region: 10%

2. Utilization Metrics

Metric	Target
CPU utilization	>70%
Memory usage	>80%
Storage efficiency	>75%
Network utilization	>65%

16.2 Optimization Strategies

Infrastructure Optimization

1. Compute Optimization

Compute Strategy:

- **Instance Selection:**

- On-demand: Critical workloads
- Spot instances: Batch training
- Reserved: Baseline loads

- **Scaling Policies:**
  - Auto-scaling:
    - Scale-up threshold: 80%
    - Scale-down threshold: 40%
    - Cool-down period: 5 minutes
- **Resource Allocation:**
  - Right-sizing: CPU optimization, memory tuning, GPU utilization

2. Storage Optimization

Storage Management:

- **Data Lifecycle Policies:**
  - Hot tier: 30 days
  - Warm tier: 90 days
  - Cold tier: 1 year
  - Archive: >1 year
- **Compression Strategy:**
  - Raw data: 2:1 ratio
  - Processed data: 3:1 ratio
  - Log files: 5:1 ratio
  - Backups: 4:1 ratio
- **Retention Rules:**
  - Business critical: 7 years
  - Operational: 2 years
  - Development: 6 months
  - Temporary: 30 days

Model Optimization

1. Training Optimization

Training Efficiency:

- **Hardware Utilization:**
    - GPU optimization: Batch size tuning, mixed precision, memory management
- **Training Strategy:**
    - Efficiency Methods: Transfer learning, progressive training, early stopping
- **Resource Scheduling:**
    - Workload Management: Peak avoidance, batch scheduling, resource sharing

2. Inference Optimization

Inference Strategy:

- **Model Serving Methods:**
    - Model quantization, batch inference, caching strategy, load balancing
- **Scaling Rules:**
    - Minimum instances: 2
    - Maximum instances: 10
    - Scale trigger: 75% CPU
    - Cool-down: 3 minutes
- **Cost Controls:**
    - Request throttling, queue management, resource limits, budget alerts

16.3 Cost Management Systems

Monitoring Framework

1. Cost Monitoring

Monitoring System:

- **Real-time Monitoring:**

    - Metrics: Usage tracking, cost accumulation, trend analysis, alert thresholds
- **Budget Controls:**
    - Management: Budget allocation, spending limits, alert systems, override procedures
- **Reporting:**
    - Analytics: Cost breakdown, usage patterns, efficiency metrics, ROI analysis

2. Alert Framework

Alert System:

- **Cost Alerts:**
    - Thresholds:
        - 80% budget consumed
        - Unusual spending patterns
        - Resource spikes
        - Trend deviations
- **Response Actions:**
    - Investigation triggers, automatic scaling, resource limits, manual review

Cost Allocation

1. Allocation Framework

Cost Distribution:

- **Department Allocation:**
    - Cost Centers: Research & Development, Production Systems, Business Units, Support Services
- **Project Allocation:**
    - Attribution: Direct costs, shared resources, overhead allocation, support costs

2. Chargeback System

Billing Framework:

- **Usage Tracking:**
  - Metrics: Compute hours, storage usage, API calls, network transfer
- **Rate Cards:**
  - Pricing: Internal rates, external rates, volume discounts, special projects
- **Billing Cycles:**
  - Schedule: Monthly reconciliation, quarterly review, annual planning, budget adjustments

16.4 Continuous Optimization

Optimization Process

1. Review Cycle

Review Framework:

- **Weekly Review:**
  - Activities: Usage patterns, cost trends, efficiency metrics, quick wins
- **Monthly Analysis:**
  - Tasks: Detailed cost review, resource optimization, performance analysis, recommendations
- **Quarterly Planning:**
  - Actions: Strategic review, budget planning, technology updates, process improvement

2. Improvement Process

Optimization Loop:

- **Analysis Phase:**

    - Steps: Data collection, pattern analysis, cost modeling, opportunity identification
- **Implementation:**
    - Actions: Priority setting, change management, deployment planning, result tracking
- **Validation:**
    - Checks: Cost impact, performance impact, user experience, ROI calculation

Chapter Summary

- Cost structure analysis
- Resource optimization strategies
- Model efficiency improvements
- Cost management frameworks
- Continuous optimization processes

Chapter 17: The Final Stretch – Bringing It All Together

As we conclude our journey through the **AI Project Playbook: From Concept to Deployment**, it's time to step back and see how all the pieces come together. AI projects are not just technical undertakings; they are strategic initiatives that intertwine innovation, operational excellence, and ethical foresight. This final chapter synthesizes the key themes of the playbook, offering a cohesive view of what it takes to turn AI ambitions into measurable success.

The Integrated AI Lifecycle

AI projects, at their core, involve a series of interconnected phases. From defining a problem to maintaining a deployed system, each stage builds on the previous one. Here's a quick recap of the lifecycle we've covered:

1. **Inception and Strategy:** Identifying business opportunities and aligning them with AI's potential.
2. **Data Preparation:** Building robust pipelines and ensuring high-quality, governed data.
3. **Model Development:** Experimenting with algorithms and evaluating performance.
4. **Deployment:** Scaling and integrating models into production environments.
5. **Monitoring and Optimization:** Continuously evaluating performance and ensuring reliability.
6. **Governance and Compliance:** Embedding ethical principles and adhering to regulatory standards.

These phases are iterative, often requiring teams to revisit earlier steps as the project evolves. By adopting a holistic approach, you ensure that each stage contributes to the overarching goal of delivering business value.

Bridging the Gaps

Throughout this playbook, we've addressed some of the most common challenges in AI projects:

- **Misaligned Objectives:** We emphasized the importance of clear, measurable goals that resonate with business priorities.
- **Data Challenges:** We outlined practical strategies for handling messy, incomplete, or biased datasets.
- **Model Deployment Hurdles:** From tooling to scalability, we've tackled the operational aspects of moving from prototype to production.
- **Ethical Dilemmas:** Governance and transparency have been central themes, reflecting AI's broader impact on society.

By addressing these pain points head-on, you can avoid the pitfalls that derail so many AI projects and ensure that your efforts drive meaningful outcomes.

Preparing for the Future

The AI landscape is rapidly evolving. New algorithms, tools, and use cases emerge daily, reshaping what's possible. To remain competitive and innovative, you must adopt a forward-looking mindset:

- **Stay Curious:** Keep exploring new technologies and methodologies.
- **Invest in Talent:** Build multidisciplinary teams that combine technical expertise with strategic insight.
- **Embrace Adaptability:** Be ready to pivot as business needs, data landscapes, and technological capabilities evolve.
- **Cultivate Ethical AI:** As AI's societal impact grows, responsible implementation will become a key differentiator.

The future of AI belongs to those who not only master its technicalities but also its human and organizational dimensions.

About the Author

Ikwe Gideon is a seasoned BI Report Developer/Analyst with over a decade of experience in retail, technology, and telecommunications sectors. He holds a Master of Science in Data Science and Analytics from Cardiff University and is a Microsoft Certified Power BI Data Analyst Associate.

Currently serving as the Manager of Data and Business Intelligence at Shop City Marketplace Limited, Gideon has a proven track record of implementing data-driven solutions that drive business growth and operational efficiency. His expertise spans data analysis, business intelligence, risk management, and advanced analytics using tools such as Azure Cloud, SQL, and Power BI.

Gideon is also the author of several books on data analytics and leadership, including "Data-Driven Logistics Revolution" and "Leadership in the Age of Data." His passion for sharing knowledge and empowering others in the field of data science is evident in his writing and professional endeavors.

With certifications in Azure Fundamentals and as an Associate Chartered Accountant, Gideon brings a unique blend of financial acumen and technical expertise to his work in data science and analytics.

www.ingramcontent.com/pod-product-compliance
Lightning Source LLC
Chambersburg PA
CBHW071003050326
40689CB00014B/3477
* 9 7 9 8 3 0 3 0 9 8 1 4 5 *